Praise for *A Deeper*

In his latest book, *A Deeper Walk*, Dr. Marcus Warner clearly, succinctly, and systematically illustrates why I consider him to be not only an excellent Bible teacher but also a world-class discipleship trainer. There is a difference between the two. I have sat under and read the works of many fine Bible teachers who knew absolutely nothing about discipleship training, but I have never sat under nor read the works of a discipleship trainer who was not also a very capable Bible teacher. We need more discipleship trainers who share not only accurate content but also Bible skills, ministry skills and life skills. This book represents both accurate Bible teaching and transferable discipleship training. It is written in a way that can be easily understood and shared with others in a Matthew 28:18–20 and 2 Timothy 2:2 methodology and manner. The numerous acronyms explained throughout the book alone represent a gold mine of information that can be easily understood and shared. Whether your interest is in learning more about spiritual warfare and freedom in Christ, or systematic discipleship training that goes beyond fill-in-the-blank clichés, this book is worth the treasure and time you invest to purchase it and read it. It is a privilege to lock arms with you in ministry to each other and others. Well done my brother; keep on!

KARL I. PAYNE
Pastor, teacher, discipleship trainer, and author

Marcus has the sacred ability to turn theological vagaries into clear and implementable opportunities for health. In *A Deeper Walk*, Marcus clarifies the oft-mistaught themes of freedom through warfare and inner healing. His teaching is vitally important because of his trusted understanding of our identity in Christ. I'm so grateful to get to endorse my friend.

JOHN LYNCH
Coauthor of *The Cure* and author of *On My Worst Day*

In his book *A Deeper Walk*, my good friend and former board member of RIMI, Dr. Marcus Warner, has identified key elements of a heart-focused discipleship. As you read through this book, you will learn about the F.I.S.H. model and receive practical tools to apply these principles to your own life and the lives of others. Together, these will help break through those seemingly impenetrable brick walls in our journey with Christ. I highly recommend this relevant work to everyone who is interested to be a serious disciple and called to go and make disciples. Please get your copy today!

SAJI LUKOS
Founder/President of RIMI Mission India / Mission India Theological Seminary

If you desire a deeper level of maturity in your walk with God, read this book! Dr. Marcus Warner shows the best model is heart-focused discipleship. There is freedom and healing in these pages.

CHRIS FABRY
Author, radio host of *Chris Fabry Live*

In *A Deeper Walk*, Marcus has managed to gather together the most significant, coherent, and powerful design to help us develop exactly what the title calls for: a deeper walk with God. All of Marcus's books are excellent, but this is his best and most comprehensive work—not only laying out what the key components of healthy discipleship are, but also presenting how to apprehend them in life. I plan on putting this in the hands of all the clergy I oversee, and all the new bishops I work with overseas.

BILL ATWOOD
Bishop, Anglican Church

A Deeper Walk is a refreshing, invigorating read by the illustrious Dr. Marcus Warner, a wellspring of wisdom and knowledge! Here we have a magnificent manifesto developed from a lifetime of study and experience in God's Word, God's character, and God's creation. In *A Deeper Walk*, Marcus works in his sweet spot, simplifying complex topics and making the Bible, God, and the Christian life clear and compelling. Marcus shines light on the essentials needed to develop a vibrant faith. Every seminary, school, and small group must read, apply, teach, live, and share this book. You will want to read this several times over and give copies to everyone you know!

CHRIS M. COURSEY
Author of *The Joy Switch* and president of THRIVEtoday

When our Christian life underperforms, we are always missing a key element. *A Deeper Walk* identifies what we are missing. Dr. Warner gives clear guidance for adding what we needed. You will be surprised at what you learn and soon be giving copies of *A Deeper Walk* to your friends.

JIM WILDER
Neurotheologian with Life Model Works and author of several books including *The Other Half of Church* (with Michel Hendricks) and *Rare Leadership* (with Marcus Warner)

This book provides a proven discipleship path to a deeper walk with God, a path that Dr. Marcus Warner brilliantly guides his readers to follow. If you long to move from just head knowledge to heart focused discipleship, *A Deeper Walk* is a must-read. In his signature way of teaching, Marcus provides accessible and practical ways to apply the truths in this book to your own life and ministry.

JUDY DUNAGAN
Author of *The Loudest Roar: Living in the Unshakable Victory of Christ* and board member of Deeper Walk International

Dr. Marcus Warner has a unique gift of communicating simply, profoundly, and memorably. This book does exactly that. He defines not only what a "deeper walk" with God means, but what the barriers to a deeper walk are. Especially important is the fact that this book recognizes and addresses the discipleship barriers for the deeply wounded and those who have experienced trauma. I love that Dr. Warner knows how to share biblical, faith-driven material alongside sound psychological principles and a sophisticated (yet understandable) description of how God made our brains to work. I would give this book to family, friends, church leaders, and clients to help deepen conversation and deepen our walk with God in our communities, in ourselves, and in our spheres of influence.

GEREMY F. KEETON
Senior Director of Counseling Service Dept., Focus on the Family

Marcus has written a phenomenal book that explains what true, biblical discipleship is meant to accomplish: creating joyful followers of Jesus who, through the overflow of their love for God, help others to discover who God is and what He's really like. With grace and humility, he explores how the culture of the church is harmed by the lack of emotional and relational maturity that living and loving like Jesus requires, while offering proven ways to understand what a Spirit-led life looks like. This book is a refreshing reminder of the fact that our secret mistrust of God hinders every aspect of our lives. But he doesn't leave us there. Marcus provides a pathway to joy to help us to understand God's plan for deliverance by His Spirit, for our good and God's glory.

JUNI FELIX
Author of *You Are Worth the Work* and member of Dr. BJ Fogg's Stanford Behavior Design Teaching Team

Our mission from the resurrected Lord is to make disciples. How are we doing? How effective are we? This book will help expand our vision of what discipleship is and equip us with better tools for engaging in the process. I deeply appreciate the way Marcus Warner discusses the importance of developing emotional and relational maturity as part of the process and how he takes the reality of demonic opposition seriously. There is much wisdom to be gained through this book that will sharpen our ability to fulfill our Lord's commission to us.

CLINTON E. ARNOLD
Research Professor of New Testament Talbot School of Theology (Biola University)

A
DEEPER
WALK

A PROVEN PATH FOR DEVELOPING
A MORE VIBRANT FAITH

MARCUS WARNER

MOODY PUBLISHERS

CHICAGO

Edited by Ashleigh Slater
Interior design: Ragont Design
Cover design: Thinkpen Design
Cover illustration of trees and cliff copyright © 2021 by patrimonio / Deposit Photos (447386532). All rights reserved.
Interior images of hand-drawn crowned heart designed by tartila / Freepik and image of hand designed by macrovector / Freepik.

All websites listed herein are accurate at the time of publication but may change in the future or cease to exist. The listing of website references and resources does not imply publisher endorsement of the site's entire contents. Groups and organizations are listed for informational purposes, and listing does not imply publisher endorsement of their activities.

ISBN: 978-0-8024-2871-4

Originally delivered by fleets of horse-drawn wagons, the affordable paperbacks from D. L. Moody's publishing house resourced the church and served everyday people. Now, after more than 125 years of publishing and ministry, Moody Publishers' mission remains the same—even if our delivery systems have changed a bit. For more information on other books (and resources) created from a biblical perspective, go to www.moodypublishers.com or write to:

Moody Publishers
820 N. LaSalle Boulevard
Chicago, IL 60610

1 3 5 7 9 10 8 6 4 2

Printed in the United States of America

To my father, Dr. Timothy M. Warner, who passed away
at the age of ninety-seven during the last weeks of working
on this book. He was the pioneer who launched me on this path.
He was my father, my mentor, and my friend.

CONTENTS

FOREWORD

THE LATE DR. TIMOTHY WARNER and I first met at a Power Evangelism Symposium sponsored by Fuller Theological Seminary. We were invited because we were teaching a course on spiritual warfare at our respective seminaries. Formal papers were presented with formal responses, which were published in a book entitled *Wrestling with Dark Angels*. At the time, I was a professor at Talbot School of Theology, and Tim was on the faculty of Trinity Evangelical Seminary. After hearing my presentation, Tim invited me to teach a doctor of ministry class at Trinity. He attended the entire class, being the humble servant he was. As a result, he decided to leave Trinity and become the International Director of Freedom in Christ Ministries and stayed with us until the Lord took him home. I have been blessed to have such a friend and colleague for many years.

Marcus would later attend a similar class I taught while working on his doctorate at Trinity Evangelical Divinity School. I share this because Marcus was the beneficiary of his father's legacy, which he has built and expanded upon. I know that Tim would be proud of what his son has accomplished. Standing on the shoulders of those who came before us and passing the mantle on to the next generation is what ministry is all about.

Knowing who we are in Christ and what it means to be a child of God in the context of a biblical worldview is what our ministries have in common. Marcus shines the light of biblical truth on today's problems in a practical way. The church is under the mandate to make disciples who can reproduce themselves. To accomplish that, we have to set captives free and heal the wounds of the brokenhearted. Every believer needs to be established alive and free in Christ so they can become the person God created them to be. That is what this book is about, and you will be better equipped to be an instrument in God's hand if you care fully apply the message.

DR. NEIL T. ANDERSON
Founder and President Emeritus of Freedom in Christ Ministries

MY STORY

I REMEMBER THE NIGHT God called me to do something about the state of discipleship in the church. It was the late 1970s, and I was in high school.

My family and I attended a traditional church with wooden pews, stained glass windows, an expensive pipe organ, and a balcony. I could usually count on being in church four times every week—Sunday school, Sunday morning worship, Sunday evening worship, and midweek prayer meeting.

By most standards, I attended a good church. We believed the Bible was the inerrant Word of God. Our pastor preached from the Bible every Sunday. We even had a Bible college across the street, so we had many well-educated Sunday school teachers. Our worship service often featured an excellent robed choir, a small orchestra, a grand piano, and of course, the pipe organ.

One evening, I stood in the balcony watching people arrive for the Sunday evening service. There was nothing out of the ordinary about this particular night. However, as I watched all the usual people file into their usual pews and the casual chitchat among old friends, a surprising thought came to my mind: "How is it possible for so many people to go to church for so many years and still seem so far away from the abundant life Christ promised?"

I somehow understood that the discipleship system in the church was broken—and I wanted to fix it.

This thought was followed by the sinking feeling that I might be looking at my future if I didn't do something. I could envision spending my whole life attending church only to miss out on all that God really had for me

That night God stirred something inside me. While I didn't know yet what the specific problems were within my church, I somehow understood that the discipleship system in it, and the church as a whole, was broken—and I wanted to fix it. But I was only eighteen at the time, and I had no idea how to do this. I just knew I couldn't keep going the way I was going, and the church couldn't afford to stay on the path it was on. Things needed to change.

THE ROAD OF ACADEMIA

Since that night, I have had a long and unusual journey. I pursued all of the formal education for ministry, but how I accomplished it was anything but typical because, in many ways, God made it easy for me.

My dad was on the faculty of every school I attended, so I feel like God just gave me my education. My father was the president of Fort Wayne Bible College, where I got a BA with an emphasis in Greek. My dad then took a position as School of World Missions and Evangelism director at Trinity Evangelical Divinity School. That was perfect because I already planned to attend that seminary when I graduated from Fort Wayne. While working on my MDiv at Trinity, I spent a year as a full-time intern at my home church, where I got to see how ministry worked from the inside out. It was a great year filled with a lot of joyful relational connections. It also further fueled my desire to improve how the church made disciples.

As I approached graduation from Trinity, I stopped in to talk to my favorite Hebrew professor. I told him I was about to graduate but was only twenty-four years old and didn't feel ready to pastor a church.

He asked, "If you could do anything you wanted to do, what would it be?" Without hesitation, I answered, "I would teach Old Testament at a Christian college."

He smiled and looked at his desk. Sitting there was a letter from Bethel College in Mishawaka, Indiana. It was a sister school to the college I had attended. They were looking for someone who could teach Old Testament for one year while one of their professors went on sabbatical.

It was clearly a God moment. The professor recommended me to Bethel, and just a few weeks later, I interviewed for the position. Bethel's president was a friend of my father's, and my interview went something like this: "If you are half the man your father is, I want you." That got me in the door. I had one of the best years of my life teaching Old Testament and systematic theology and pouring into the lives of many of the students on campus.

As it happened, the professor on sabbatical decided not to come back. So, I ended up teaching at Bethel for three years. That was just long enough for me to start dating my future wife, Brenda Schlabach. We've now been married for over thirty years, and she has been a wonderful partner in every way imaginable.

At that point in my journey, I planned to be a professor for the rest of my life. The path forward seemed obvious. Get a PhD in Old Testament and hope a door would open to return to Bethel. However, God had been operating in another part of my life for several years and had other plans.

FROM SCHOLAR TO MINISTER OF WOUNDED HEARTS

My parents had developed a reputation for spiritual warfare ministry. In fact, my father taught the most popular elective at Trinity. It was related to power encounters on the mission field, but the course also dealt with personal issues and helped students understand how to apply spiritual warfare to battles in their own lives.[1]

After a few years, my dad invited Dr. Neil T. Anderson to come from Talbot School of Theology and teach the doctoral students at Trinity for a week. My dad attended the classes, and by the end of it, he decided it was time to leave academia and go into freedom work full-time. He joined Dr. Anderson's new organization, Freedom in Christ Ministries.

Shortly after this, I began working with my parents and quickly got involved in the world of spiritual warfare and emotional healing. By the time I was in my mid thirties, I had probably met with a hundred people and had helped with a few who had some of the most horrific stories of childhood abuse imaginable. Many of

I sensed God calling me to step away from academia and minister to wounded hearts.

these people had multiple personalities, as we called it then.

One night, a group of us were up until almost two in the morning dealing with demons and praying as Jesus amazingly met one of these people and healed a very painful memory. It was utterly amazing to watch someone switch from hating God to loving Jesus in about twenty minutes because of the healing they received.

The next day, I sat in a doctoral class translating and discussing the rabbis whose commentaries are found in the Talmud. If that seems a bit dry and academic, it was. The contrast between the academic work I was doing and the emotional healing work of the night before weighed heavily on me. At that moment, I had another clear, distinct, and surprising thought: "I did not call you to be a scholar. I called you to minister to wounded hearts."

God was once again preparing me for a new stage of life. My wife had just informed me that our first child was on the way, and it became clear that my life in the academic world was winding down. I switched majors, and the seminary awarded me a master of theology degree in Old Testament for the work I had already done, plus a few extra requirements.

Over the next twenty years, I spent time teaching in Christian schools and pastoring in local churches, but God kept sending me deeply wounded people who needed help throughout it all. It was a journey I did not expect. Along the way, I met some great mentors and colleagues who helped me grow in my understanding of how people change. I learned more about spiritual warfare, inner healing, walking in the Spirit, and then—surprisingly—about brain science and attachment theory.

In 2006, I became the president of what is now Deeper Walk International. This ministry had a strong relationship with Dr. E. James (Jim) Wilder, who had led a team to develop a neuroscience-based model of maturity development. Jim and I became friends, and I began to quickly learn all I could from him about the brain and maturity. We eventually wrote three books together: *Rare Leadership*, *The Solution of Choice*, and *Rare Leadership in the Workplace*. I also wrote two books with Chris Coursey, who had been mentored by Jim and applied neuroscience to relational skill development. Chris and I wrote *The 4 Habits of Joy-Filled Marriages* and *The 4 Habits of Raising Joy-Filled Kids*.

A NEW AND HOLISTIC DISCIPLESHIP MODEL

As you can see, my journey took me in some unexpected directions. But, as a result of this winding path, God brought all the pieces together as He led me to a holistic model of discipleship. I call this model heart-focused discipleship, and it is built on five core elements of the gospel—freedom, identity, Spirit, heart-focused community, and mission. When you bring these elements together, they create a clear path to a deeper walk with God.

The goal of this book is to meet you where you are to help you develop a new level of maturity in your walk with God. This isn't a path I invented. Many have walked this road before us. This is a tested path. It is a proven path, and I am confident that following this path will help you experience a deeper and more vibrant walk with God.

CHAPTER 1

HALF-BRAINED CHRISTIANITY

AS I SAT ON A STREET CORNER one cold, Chicago night, I remember thinking, "If this is all there is to Christianity, maybe I should look into something else."

I was discouraged. I had spent my whole life going to church. I attended private Christian schools, went to a Bible college, and I was in seminary preparing for ministry. If anyone understood Christianity, I figured it was me. The problem was that after all these years, I still felt like I was missing something important. I rarely felt close to God, and I was acutely aware of the enormous gap between the life I lived and the "abundant" life Christ promised (John 10:10). It was not that I never had good days. It was just that I had way too many days where I felt like I was just going through the motions.

Part of my problem was that I was the product of traditional discipleship, or what I sometimes call *half-brained Christianity*. I call it that because traditional discipleship is extremely left-brained in its focus. It stresses truth, choices, and discipline as keys to successful Christian

living. It also emphasizes the importance of volunteering and evangeliz-
ing, but it doesn't really address matters of the heart.

Traditional discipleship tends to outsource issues of the heart to
professional counselors. I grew up in a generation of pastors who are in-
clined to see themselves as teachers and leaders, but who see counseling
as something for specialists. We were trained how to teach the Bible well
and prepare relevant sermons on topics that touched the heart, but most
of us have no idea how to build a church

Traditional discipleship falls short of offering us the solutions we need to handle heart-level issues.

that offers people solutions beyond traditional discipleship. I remember one pastor
of a large and prosperous church saying,
"I feel like my congregation is a boiling
pot of emotional issues. If I even hinted
that we could help people with their deep
issues, I fear the pot would boil over. We
would end up creating a mess that would
be impossible to clean up."[1] I don't blame
the pastors as much as I blame a system that sees traditional discipleship
as adequate.

In this opening chapter, I want to explain in more depth what traditional discipleship is and why it falls short of offering us the solutions we
need to handle heart-level issues.

DISCIPLESHIP BY OSMOSIS

When my father was teaching at Trinity Evangelical Divinity School, he
had a student turn in a paper in which he shared the following testimony:

> I have never been discipled, and I have been a Christian for twenty
> years. Because of not knowing who I am in Christ, I did not know
> how to walk according to the Spirit. Therefore, I have been living
> my life according to the flesh while gaining a lot of head knowledge
> about the Bible and God.

I have struggled so long because of my weakness to say no to myself, and I have really been ineffective for Christ. I was always told by those I opened up to what to do, but it never had any power in my life. I know a lot of theology, and I know everything I should do, but I do not bear much fruit, and I do not love others the way God wants me to.

I feel like a baby Christian because I have to start at the basics again and reprogram my faulty ways of thinking. I have grown up with a poor self-esteem, self-condemnation, self-hatred, bitterness, rebellion, perfectionism, anxiety, and a weak functional faith.[2]

Clearly, this young man was ready for a different kind of Christianity. He was ready to go deeper than where traditional discipleship could take him. He was looking for heart-focused discipleship—which I'll explain in detail in the next chapter.

He is not the only one who struggles. In a well-known report issued by the Willow Creek Association, it was suggested that as many as 25 percent of church members describe their walk with God as stalled or dissatisfying.[3] In response to this report, many churches launched a back-to-basics movement and called for more discipleship in the church. The problem, from my perspective, was that too many churches responded by returning to the traditional discipleship model that had created the situation in the first place.

What further complicates the issue is that some churches don't even practice traditional discipleship well. They are stuck in a process that is something like osmosis.

Discipleship by osmosis is sort of like discipleship by assumption. It assumes that if you join the church and hang around long enough, you will get discipled. It is a bit like sticking a Spanish textbook under your pillow and hoping you will learn how to speak Spanish by having it in the area.

The process usually looks like this: You start attending a church, and after a while, someone asks you to volunteer. If you are faithful as a volunteer, you are soon asked to lead. If you are faithful as a leader, you can find yourself in the inner circle of power in that church without ever being discipled.

This scenario happened to a friend of mine. He was in full-time Christian ministry at a parachurch organization, served faithfully in the local church, and was eventually voted onto the elder board. But one day, he sat down in my office and cried as he described a life that was starting to fall apart. What he told me that day has stayed with me ever since.

He said, "I've been in the church and in full-time Christian ministry since I was in college, and I have never been discipled."

I could sense his anger and growing frustration. He knew much of what he was going through was his own fault. But he was also beginning to wonder how it was possible to get as far as he had without anyone helping him. This wonderful man was almost taken out because everyone assumed he was being discipled, when he was really just a very faithful worker. He was a victim of discipleship by osmosis.

TRADITIONAL DISCIPLESHIP

The traditional discipleship model with which I was raised stressed will power, academic training, and church activity as the keys to living a successful Christian life. So, when I talk about traditional discipleship, I often think of the ABCs of most discipleship programs: academics, behavior, and church activity.

Academics

As I shared in the introduction, I am a big fan of academics. I couldn't wait to go to Bible college and seminary. I figured I would get "super-discipled" by studying the Bible and the languages of Greek, Hebrew, Aramaic, and Latin. I looked forward to examining the church fathers and diving into scholarly debates. It did give me a wonderful foundation for which I am very grateful.

I loved learning and still love learning, but it didn't take long to realize there was a pretty big gap between my head and my heart. The Christian life is not just about thinking deep thoughts or even thinking correctly. There is something deeper going on inside the heart that academics doesn't touch. Part of my discouragement with the Christian faith was that I knew I wouldn't find the answers I was looking for in more biblical study.

> **The Christian life is not just about thinking deep thoughts or even thinking correctly. There is something deeper going on inside the heart that academics doesn't touch.**

Behavior

When study didn't produce what I was looking for, I assumed I could find it in developing a life of discipline. I knew I needed a disciplined quiet time, a disciplined prayer life, and a focus on good behavior. If I could just do good things, surely I would become a good person.

But what I found was that I never seemed to measure up. Sometimes I was super disciplined, and sometimes I felt like I had no discipline at all. No matter how much I tried, I always seemed to fall short of developing the level of discipline and good behavior I thought a true Christian should have.

So, discipline felt like a fickle solution. The harder I worked at behaving well, the more it exposed the fact that something was broken inside that kept sabotaging my efforts.

Church Activity

One of the assumptions made by the folks who produced the study from Willow Creek was that church activity would lead to maturity. It turned out that it doesn't. You can be involved in a small group, volunteer in a social justice ministry, participate in evangelistic outreaches, and still find yourself stalled and dissatisfied as a Christian.

Personally, I started teaching Sunday School when I was fourteen and basically never stopped. I've been teaching somewhere, at some level, ever since. I have also been in dozens of small groups and launched, organized, and participated in numerous programs designed to help others. What I found was that sometimes it was great, and sometimes it just wore me out and left me drained and discouraged.

I realized later that when it was great, it was because I enjoyed being with the people who were in the project with me. The more joy there was relationally, the more transformative the experience turned out to be. But joy seemed like the exception rather than the rule. Too often, church activity just turned into a duty to discharge rather than a point of deep and energizing connection.

I could go on, but I think you get the idea. Traditional disciple-ship focuses on what Jesus called "the outside of the cup" (Matt. 23:25), but it generally misses the inside. In my case, traditional discipleship left me looking really good on the outside. My résumé was impressive. Churches loved having me around because I volunteered, had experi-ence and credentials, was theologically sound, and served faithfully. The problem for me was that these things didn't necessarily translate into a deeper connection with God. There was still a gap between what I got from traditional discipleship and what I knew I needed if I wanted a more vibrant walk with God.

ASSESSING THE PROBLEM

When I was in seminary, a visiting professor asked us, "If the church was a factory, what would its product be?" After a short discussion, we all agreed that the product would be disciples. The instructor spent the rest of the course trying to help us learn how to become disciple-making pastors.

It was good material as far as it went. However, most of the assump-tions about what constituted good discipleship were built on the ABCs and getting people involved in evangelism. While that is all good stuff, it still misses something that touches on the deeper issues of the heart.

What I have learned since then was that there was a word missing in our answer. The church doesn't just exist to make disciples. We also exist to bring those disciples to *maturity*. The goal of the discipleship process is to produce *mature* disciples. This aim is in keeping with Paul's vision to "present everyone mature in Christ" (Col. 1:28) and to see every Christian grow into maturity "with a stature measured by Christ's fullness" (Eph. 4:13 CSB).

I have a friend who is an engineer. He often gets paid to help companies improve the quality of their products. He has observed that if the church really were a factory, there is no way anyone would be satisfied with the quality of the product being produced. As my friend assessed the discipleship situation in the church, he concluded that most churches don't know how to describe what a mature disciple is, or they operate with faulty growth models. Thus, they are either aiming at the wrong target or using a flawed process for reaching that target, or both.

Spiritual maturity cannot be separated from emotional and relational maturity.

What does it mean, then, to be a mature disciple of Jesus? Let's start by looking at it in more detail.

Spiritual maturity cannot be separated from emotional and relational maturity.[4] If we are looking for a measuring stick of how we know someone is mature, the fruit of the Spirit is a great place to start. Let's take a quick look at the first four. Notice how they are all related to emotional and relational skills:

- **Love**—That's about as relational as it gets.
- **Joy**—It is the anchor of emotional maturity. According to the latest neuroscience, joy determines our capacity to handle upsetting emotions.[5]
- **Peace**—Peace and joy combine to create the foundation of emotional capacity. Peace is a good description of being quieted from distressing emotions.

- **Patience**—It is core to relational maturity. One can define maturity as the ability to suffer well.[6] The Greek word makrothumia for patience means "great suffering."[7]

If we take this seriously, it means that any definition of spiritual maturity must also include emotional and relational maturity. Sadly, the church is littered with people who have gone through extensive training in traditional discipleship without growing in emotional or relational maturity.

Even countless pastors and Christian leaders have received excellent educations and have even gone through extensive discipleship training without becoming emotionally or relationally mature. They are often charismatic, talented, and visionary, but the people closest to them walk on eggshells, unsure of what will set them off next.

I don't mean to pick on pastors. I was a pastor, and I know there are lots of great people in ministry. But it makes the point. If you can reach the "pinnacle" of church leadership without actually developing maturity, is it reasonable to think our discipleship process will create maturity in others?

ASSESSING MATURITY

My friend, Jim Wilder, is a unique person who has an in-depth knowledge of Scripture and has an advanced understanding of neuroscience. Based on both Scripture and neuroscience, Jim has concluded that maturity is the ability to remain relational, act like yourself, and return to joy despite upsetting emotions. People who can do these things even when enduring hardship are truly mature. This model of maturity can be remembered with the word RARE:

- Remain relational
- Act like yourself
- Return to joy
- Endure hardship well[8]

The idea is that you can measure maturity by how much suffering it takes before someone melts down, shuts down, or blows up relationally. It takes only a little hardship for an immature individual to stop being relational and start acting like a different person. In the same way, it takes a lot to overwhelm a mature person to the point that you fear being around them.

> **Maturity is the ability to remain relational, act like yourself, and return to joy despite upsetting emotions.**

As we've talked about, too many Christians lack emotional and relational maturity. It takes relatively little stress for them to snap. People around them operate out of fear because they are never sure which person they will get— the mature adult or the emotionally immature child.

But you can tell who the most mature person is in any group by who can handle the most emotional weight and still remain relational and act like themselves. Mature people also excel at returning to joy from upsetting emotions. They are exactly the sort of people you want around when emotions are high because they exert a calming influence on the whole group.

Think about it this way: If you are in distress, who do you want to talk to? Someone who will get overwhelmed by how you feel? Probably not. Someone who will try to fix you without really understanding you? I doubt it. You want someone who can hear your distress, still be happy to be with you, and help you recover your joy, don't you? That's maturity.

The Scriptures often talk about maturity in terms of human development. It speaks of spiritual infants, children, adults, parents, and elders. Using these categories can help us assess our own maturity. Let's take a closer look.

Infants

In 1 Corinthians 3:1–2, Paul addressed the Corinthian Christians as infants in the faith. He didn't mean they lacked knowledge. He meant they lacked maturity. What he chastised them for was the immaturity that divided into factions in the name of being wise. They lacked emotional and relational maturity.

Infants cannot take care of themselves. They need someone else to do everything for them. In a spiritual sense, we are infants when we easily lose our ability to stay relational and act like ourselves and need someone else to help us recover, or we will get stuck in our distress for a long time.

It is possible to have a doctorate in ministry but be an infant emotionally and relationally. Just ask my wife. When holes in my maturity development get exposed, I can stop acting like myself and turn into a child or an infant. I don't do this as often as I used to, but when it happens, it is a clear sign that I have some growth issues that need to be addressed.

Children

Childhood is about learning the skills that we need to master to take care of our personal needs. Most children learn how to dress and feed themselves and care for themselves physically. And, when they become fully mature, they are self-sufficient. However, many do not get the same training when it comes to caring for their emotional needs or handling their relationships well. In this sense, spiritual children are good at making sure their own needs get met, but they are not good at making sure the needs of those around them are met.

People who are stuck at infant- or child-level maturity get angry easily, avoid difficult people and hard tasks, and generally find themselves struggling with some kind of addiction. Many spiritual children do their best to hide these shortcomings, so only the people closest to them see what is really going on.

A discipleship process that moves people from infant-level maturity to adult-level maturity needs to help people learn how Christians care for their hearts and recover from upsetting emotions. It should be a standard part of the discipleship process, and something we will devote a significant amount of attention to in the remainder of the book.

Adults

The focus of adults moves from taking care of only themselves to also focusing on the needs of their group or people. Paul put it this way, "Do nothing out of selfish ambition or vain conceit. Rather, in humility value others above yourselves, not looking to your own interests but each of you to the interests of the others" (Phil. 2:3–4 NIV). This is a good description of adult-level maturity.

Spiritual adults are emotionally stable and good with relationships. When a group of people are forming a committee in the church, one pastor I know often asks, "Who is the adult in the room?" He means, "Who will be in this meeting who has the ability to keep the relationships civil and the emotions from getting out of hand?"

Parents

Parents are those who have been practicing adult-level maturity for a few years and are ready to start training a new generation in the skills and habits of maturity. There was apparently a shortage of spiritual parents in Corinth. Paul wrote:

For though you have countless guides in Christ, you do not have many fathers. For I became your father in Christ Jesus through the gospel. I urge you, then, be imitators of me. That is why I sent you Timothy, my beloved and faithful child in the Lord, to remind you of my ways in Christ. (1 Cor. 4:15–17)

The Corinthians lacked people who could model adult-level maturity, so Paul sent Timothy to be a spiritual parent and help them develop their own maturity and produce even more spiritual parents capable of mentoring others. Paul did not send Timothy because the Corinthians lacked good teachers and good information, but because they lacked models of adult maturity who could train others in the kind of spiritual maturity that produced emotional and relational skills.

Elders

An elder is not just an office in the church. Elders have raised their own children and are available to care for the community. After navigating the highs and lows of parenting their kids (so that the youngest of them has become an adult), a true elder is well-practiced not only in adult maturity but in helping others fill holes in their maturity development.

There is a reason God wanted so many elders in this world. He knew we would need help navigating the hardships of a fallen world.

It is significant that in a typical lifetime, most people spend nearly half their lives as elders. If I have my first child at age twenty and see my youngest reach adulthood around age forty-five, I will spend the next forty-five years as an elder (if I live to be ninety). There is a reason God wanted so many elders in this world. He knew we would need help navigating the hardships of a fallen world. There is a reason the apostles wanted elders in positions of authority in the church. To be an elder was to be recognized by the community as someone who had raised their family and demonstrated the kind of spiritual maturity that exhibits godly character even during hardship.

DISCIPLESHIP IS MATURITY DEVELOPMENT

Every church has people at various stages of maturity, and we need spiritual parents and elders to help guide infants and children. The discipleship process is one of maturity development that meets people where they are and helps them develop the skills and habits to move to the next stage of maturity.

Understanding that maturity is the goal of the discipleship process means that the holes inherent in traditional discipleship are unacceptable. We need a discipleship process that routinely moves people from one stage of maturity to the next. In this sense, the church is not so much a factory as a family, and this process requires a growth model with a proven track record of producing mature Christians.

LOOKING AHEAD TO A GROWTH MODEL THAT WORKS

It was over thirty years ago that I felt the discouragement and sense of hopelessness as to whether Christianity really had the answers I needed. Since then, I have been on a long journey of recognizing the holes in my own maturity development and working through issues I didn't even know I had.

If the goal of the Christian faith is to learn to love God and others, it makes sense that our discipleship process should not simply be about academics, good behavior, and church activity. It should be anchored in a growth model that helps us become more loving people, who stay loving people even when life gets hard.

I am not perfect and do not have all the answers, but I am much farther down the path than I used to be. So, in the pages ahead, I will share with you a growth model that works. It's called heart-focused discipleship. It is less half-brained and more whole-brained, yet firmly rooted in the gospel. I didn't invent this model. Instead, it is a compilation of tools and perspectives that have changed lives for generations. I've just tried to make it easy to understand and simple to get started.

CHAPTER 2

HEART-FOCUSED DISCIPLESHIP

A GROUP OF MISSIONARIES made their way to a village in India. They were part of a group that offered to dig wells in rural areas to bring fresh drinking water to the people. They discovered that this village already had a well. But something had gone wrong with it, and the people had started using the well as the town dump. It was literally filled with all sorts of garbage, even broken toilets!

The missionary team discussed the matter and decided it would be more cost-effective to reclaim this well than dig a new one. So, they got to work. They started emptying all the garbage out of the shaft, which couldn't have been the most pleasant task in the world. About halfway down the well, they found something they did not expect—a cobra's nest! I'm sure someone had a mild heart attack with that discovery. The group contacted a specialist and had these poisonous snakes relocated before they finished their project.

After pressure washing the shaft, the team finally reached the bottom. Here they discovered the source of the problem: the foundation stones had collapsed and were clogging the spring. As a result, no water could enter the well. Now that they had discovered the source of the problem, they got to work and restored the foundations.

Finally, the day came when they finished. Everyone celebrated, and there were hugs all around as water from the spring refilled the well. What had started as the town dump had been reclaimed. It was now a source of life to the whole community.

When I first heard this story, I thought, "Now, that will preach!" It is a great metaphor for heart-focused discipleship. The well is like the individual who wants a deeper walk with God but feels stuck. Some people feel like they are worthless and have nothing to offer to others. But with the help of a team and by getting to root issues, their lives can be reclaimed so that they become a source of life to others.

There are five core elements to heart-focused discipleship, and they can all be seen in this story: freedom, identity, Spirit, heart-focused community, and mission. Let's look closely at each one.

1. FREEDOM

The missionaries had to clear out the junk that was clogging the well. In the same way, as Christians, we need help to get unclogged from the baggage and bondage in our lives. Just as they found cobras in the well and needed a specialist to remove them, some people also need help with spiritual warfare issues as part of their freedom work.

2. IDENTITY

The foundation of the Christian life is our identity in Christ. Bad things happen when that foundation collapses. In the same way, when we do not understand our identity in Christ or if the devil's lies rob us of that solid foundation, it can impede the flow of the Spirit within and keep us stuck. I have talked to more than one Christian counselor who has said the most common issue their clients have is not understanding their identity in Christ.

To help grasp the importance of freedom and identity, consider a story Max Lucado tells about his experience with a houseboat and a hurricane.[1] Max was from the Midwest but thought it would be fun to live on a houseboat in Florida. However, he wasn't there long before storm warnings were issued about a large hurricane heading his way. Unfamiliar with hurricanes and houseboats, he and the friends who lived with him did their best and began tying their floating home to every fixed, immovable object they could find. They tied it to palm trees and fire hydrants, and anything else that seemed secure.

Soon a man named Phil came by. He was a veteran of the sea who had weathered many such storms. Phil saw what the young men were doing and took pity on them. "You're going to tear that houseboat apart," he said.

"What do you mean?" they asked.

"When the winds hit and the water starts to surge, the ropes will simply rip your houseboat apart," he explained. "What you think is making you safe is setting you up for destruction."

"So, what do we do?"

"Anchor deep," the wise man said. "Untie yourself from all these objects on land and get yourself some long rope with plenty of slack in it. Anchor the four ropes to four secure locations on the bottom of the riverbed. Then when the wind blows, and the water goes up and down, your houseboat will bob up and down with the motion, but not get ripped apart."

> **Our journey to a deeper walk with God starts by getting free from what has us in bondage and building on the unshakable foundation of our identity in Christ.**

I love this story because it illustrates so well the importance of freedom—breaking loose from sins, habits, and beliefs we may have thought were keeping us safe—and anchoring our lives to something permanent, namely our identity in Christ. Our journey to a deeper walk with God starts by getting free from what has us in bondage and building on the unshakable foundation of our identity in Christ.

3. SPIRIT

The key to the Christian life is the Holy Spirit. Perhaps the core image of how the Christian life is to be lived comes from the parable of the vine and the branches in John 15. Jesus said, "I am the vine; you are the branches. . . . Apart from me you can do nothing" (John 15:5). The parable creates a wonderful image of what it means to be attached to Jesus. When our lives are grafted into His, it creates a connection that allows His life (through the Holy Spirit) to flow into our lives.

When we are saved, we are born of the Spirit. Our relationship with God is often summarized as *walking in the Spirit*. If the Spirit is not free to flow in our lives, we cannot bear fruit for God's kingdom. Instead, we will feel stalled and dissatisfied. In the story of the well, the water represents the Holy Spirit. Once the well was unclogged and the foundation was repaired, the water was free to flow once again.

4. HEART-FOCUSED COMMUNITY

Notice that it took a team to unclog the well. It didn't fix itself. In the same way, the journey to a deeper walk with God is not intended to be traveled alone. It is meant to be shared with others also working on their heart issues with integrity and transparency. The process gets easier when I know I am part of a group that is on the same journey.

In my own life, I have noticed that when I try to build new habits on my own, I rarely make it more than a week or two. But if I join a class and feel like I belong to a group going in the same direction, I am far better at building new habits because I don't want to let others down and I like the feeling of belonging.

Two examples jump immediately to mind. I used to play a lot of tennis. In fact, I taught tennis early in my life. But as soon as I stopped being part of a league, I quit playing. Even though I liked the sport, without the motivation of belonging to a group, it wasn't a priority for me anymore. The same thing happened with Bible memorization. When I was part of a Bible quiz team at my church, I studied up to fifteen hours a week. When I was no longer a part of the group, my motivation waned, and the practice quickly became part of my past. Whenever I tried to renew the practice on my own, I got bogged down and quit.

5. MISSION

The result of reclaiming the well was the ability to offer life-giving water to the whole village. In the same way, the goal of heart-focused discipleship is not simply to feel better. It is not merely for our healing; it is reclaiming our purpose in life so that we can do the good works God prepared in advance for us to do (Eph. 2:10).

One of my favorite verses is Acts 13:36. It says, "Now when David had served God's purpose in his own generation, he fell asleep" (NIV). It is a reminder that we all have a purpose for our lives and that God wants us to impact this generation. Sometimes we can wish we had been born at a different time in history when things were easier, but God has a reason for where He puts us. As we grow in our walk with God, it will naturally lead us into God's purpose for our lives, and that purpose will always involve being part of a mission bigger than ourselves.

BIBLICAL FOUNDATIONS OF
HEART-FOCUSED DISCIPLESHIP

Several years ago, I was teaching on Romans 5–8 for a group of pastors in the Pacific Northwest. As we walked through the text together, we asked one basic question, "What does Paul say is essential to a victorious Christian life?" By the time we were done, we had landed on three essentials, with which everyone agreed.

1. Freedom

Paul wrote that we died with Christ, which set us free from the law and sin. As we read in Romans 6:6–7, "For we know that our old self was crucified with him [Christ] so that the body ruled by sin might be done away with, that we should no longer be slaves to sin—because anyone who has died *has been set free* from sin" (NIV, emphasis added). He then told us to reckon ourselves "dead to sin but alive to God" (Rom. 6:11 NIV). In other words, Christ set us free to walk in freedom. Thus, we agreed that helping people learn how to experience freedom is an essential element of a transformational discipleship process.

> **Helping people learn how to experience freedom is an essential element of a transformational discipleship process.**

2. Identity

Paul wrote that we were raised with Christ (Eph. 2:6; Col. 2:12; 3:1). Our resurrection with Christ opened the door to a new life as God's adopted children (Rom. 8:15). In Romans 8:12–17, Paul spent a good bit of time talking about our adoption into God's family and the inheritance that came with our adoption. It doesn't take much to see that understanding our new identity in Christ is a second essential element of a deeper walk.

3. Spirit

Paul summarized the difference between a successful life in Christ and a struggling life in Christ as the difference between walking in the Spirit and walking in the flesh. We read in Romans 8:12–13, "So then, brothers, we are debtors, not to the flesh, to live according to the flesh. For if you live according to the flesh you will die, but if by the Spirit you put to death the deeds of the body, you will live." Statements like this made it easy to agree that Spirit-filled living is essential to a victorious Christian life.

In Romans 8:15–18, Paul brought all three of these ideas together—freedom, identity, and Spirit—when he wrote:

> The Spirit you received does not make you slaves [freedom], so that you live in fear again; rather, the Spirit you received brought about your adoption to sonship [identity]. And by him we cry, "Abba, Father." The Spirit himself testifies with our spirit that we are God's children. Now if we are children, then we are heirs—heirs of God and co-heirs with Christ, if indeed we share in his sufferings in order that we may also share in his glory." (NIV)

Notice how Paul stressed freedom, identity, and the Spirit as core to growing maturity. Remember from chapter one that maturity is related to suffering well. Paul pointed us in this direction in this passage when he calls us to share in Christ's sufferings so that we may also share in His glory.

The pastors in this meeting all agreed that if Paul were going to build a transformational discipleship ministry, it would be anchored in the principles of freedom, identity, and life in the Spirit. And yet—based on a show of hands—none of them had a strategic plan for doing this. No one had a freedom ministry in their church. None of them had a repeatable process for teaching people their identity in Christ. None of them could raise their hand and say, "We have a clear process for explaining what it means to walk in the Spirit and how to do it."

The problem was not that these were bad pastors. Every one of them was deeply committed to discipleship. Each longed to see their people experiencing a deeper walk with God and a more vibrant faith. The problem was that they had all been trained in traditional discipleship. Despite going to college, seminary, and numerous training events, no one had ever helped them catch the vision for something so clearly taught in the Bible. Every pastor in the room agreed that if I could give them a model for implementing this type of discipleship, they would put it into practice.

HEART-FOCUSED COMMUNITY

Since the day I spent with that group of pastors, I have come to realize that there is one other crucial element Paul taught about how to experience a vibrant walk with God, and that is heart-focused community. As you read Romans 5–8, you begin to notice that Paul constantly used the word "we." He was writing to a group and telling them, "This is who we are. This is how it is like us to do things." In fact, in most of Paul's letters, Paul appealed to our group identity as believers. We are God's elect (Col. 3:12). We have been bought with a price and belong to Jesus (1 Cor. 6:20; 7:23). We are deeply loved (Col. 3:12). We are heirs of an eternal inheritance (Rom. 8:17). The list goes on. On the basis of our group identity, what Paul wrote encourages us to live in a manner worthy of the calling we have received (Eph. 4:1).

> **While there are many things we can do as individuals to spur our growth, the journey itself is meant to be taken as a people, together.**

Paul also modeled heart-focused community in his ministry. He routinely traveled in a group, and established communities wherever he went that functioned like extended families. While there are many things we can do as individuals to spur our growth, the journey itself is meant to be taken as a people, together.

BACK TO THE WELL

You can think of your own life in terms of the well story I shared. If you want to go deeper in your walk with God and experience a more vibrant life with Him, heart-focused discipleship provides a proven pathway to get you there. As the story suggests, it will take some work, but the results are more than worth the effort.

In the next chapter, we will look at this model more closely. Then, in the pages after it, you will learn practical tools and perspectives to help you on this journey.

CHAPTER 3

DISCIPLESHIP ON THE BACK OF A NAPKIN

WHEN I WAS IN HIGH SCHOOL, I was taught how to draw the bridge diagram as a tool for explaining the gospel. This model was sometimes called "evangelism on the back of a napkin," because you could easily draw the diagram on a napkin or scrap piece of paper. If you are not familiar with the bridge diagram, it looks like this:

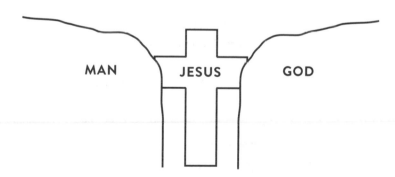

MAN   JESUS   GOD

The idea of this illustration is that sin has created a huge gulf between God and man. There is nothing man can do from his side to bridge this gap. No matter how good we try to be, we all fall short (Rom. 3:23). Knowing this, God built a bridge to us. He sent Jesus into the world to die for our sins. We simply need to acknowledge our need and receive the gift in order to cross the bridge and be saved.

As a pastor, I used this diagram dozens of times to lead people into a relationship with God. Sometimes, I literally drew it on the back of a napkin. However, I usually added something to it. After the diagram, I would draw a question mark and ask, "So what comes next? What happens if you cross this bridge? What changes?"

My answer to these questions usually looked something like this:

- **First, I would draw a picture of a scroll to represent the new covenant.** Then, I would explain that crossing the bridge meant entering a covenant relationship with God. It is like entering a marriage covenant. Getting married changes who you are. You stop being a single person and become a married couple. If you keep acting like a single person after your identity changes, bad things are going to happen. In the same way, the new covenant transforms you from a sinner into a saint, from a stranger into a son or daughter of God. It defines your relationship with God so that you can know exactly where you stand with Him. Entering a new covenant relationship with God changes your identity and establishes the foundation for a whole new life.
- **Next, I would sometimes draw a crown and explain that the new covenant does more than just change our identity.** It also guarantees an inheritance in heaven. What you do with the rest of your life determines how big that inheritance will be, but the new covenant makes you part of the family and an heir of God's kingdom. Part of our motivation to lead godly lives is the promise of an inheritance to come.
- **Finally, I often drew a picture of a bird to represent the Holy Spirit.** I told people that the new covenant created a legal

arrangement that defined our relationship with God. It adopted us into the family and gave us an inheritance. But there is more than just legality to our walk with God. We are not merely adopted; we are also born again (John 3:3). Adoption happens in the new covenant. To be born again is to receive the Holy Spirit (John 3:5). It is described as being born of the Spirit (John 3:6). Christianity can be summed up in one sentence: We are born of the Spirit to live in the Spirit.

The new covenant transforms you from a sinner into a saint, from a stranger into a son or daughter.

By the time I shared all of this, nearly everyone had said yes to God and prayed to receive Christ. Of course, most of them had come to me looking for answers, so I was working with people who were active seekers. I am not saying this is a magic formula for getting people saved, just that knowing "the rest of the story" seemed to help them decide.

BAPTISM AND THE FISH MODEL

Most churches are pretty good at explaining the bridge diagram or something like it. However, far fewer churches have a simple tool for explaining the pathway to a deeper walk with God. In this chapter, I want to introduce you to the FISH diagram. The word FISH is anchored in the experience of baptism. (Perhaps you can think of fish swimming in the baptismal waters). It is intended to help you remember four essential elements of a deeper walk with God:

- Freedom
- Identity
- Spirit
- Heart-focused community

If the bridge diagram can be called "evangelism on the back of a napkin," the FISH diagram can be called "discipleship on the back of a napkin." The diagram looks like this:

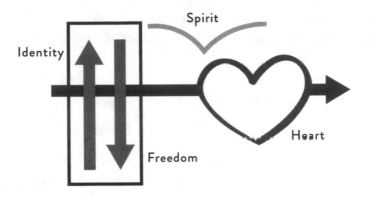

Imagine you are sitting in a coffee shop, and you want to explain heart-focused discipleship to the person you are with. Where do you start? Here is a simple model.

You begin by drawing a straight line on the back of napkin. This line represents the water of baptism.

After we say yes to God and receive Christ, baptism is the ceremony that marks our entry into the Christian community. It symbolizes the washing away of sin and much more. There are many different approaches to baptism. Some churches baptize infants, some baptize by sprinkling water on a person, and some baptize by dunking people completely underwater. The last method creates the clearest picture that we are dying with Christ to our old identity and being raised to a new identity as a member of God's family in baptism. Baptism does not save us in the sense that merely going through the ritual guarantees us a place in heaven. However, baptism was widely understood in the early church as the sign that you had left your old life and joined Christ's kingdom family.

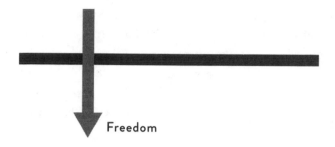

Freedom

Next, you draw an arrow pointing down and through the line. This arrow represents the idea that when we enter the water of baptism, we are dying with Christ to our old life. The idea of dying with Christ means there is a clear break from our past life. A crucial part of discipleship moving forward is related to putting off the old patterns that we learned in our old lives. We need to put off lies we have believed, sin that has enslaved us, and bitterness that has kept us in bondage. Death may seem harsh, but it is important. Only by dying to the old patterns of living can we be free from them. To reinforce this, you might write the word "freedom" next to the downward pointing arrow.

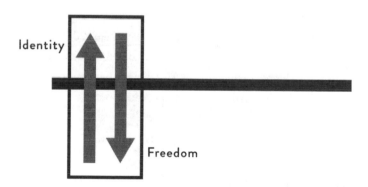

Identity

Freedom

Next to the downward arrow, you draw an arrow that is pointing up and through the line of baptism. This arrow represents the idea that we have been raised with Christ to a new identity. The old person died with Christ, and a new one is raised in his place. This provides an opportunity to explain that an important part of the discipleship process is learning to understand our new identity in Christ. Just as joining the Army would mean that we die to our civilian identity in order to live as a soldier, so joining our lives to Christ means learning to understand and embrace all that changes by belonging to Him. To reinforce this point, it may help to write the word "identity" next to the second arrow.

A big part of our journey involves putting off the old and putting on the new as we learn to live a life worthy of the calling we have received.

At this point, I sometimes draw a box around these two arrows and explain that the box represents the new covenant. I briefly mentioned the new covenant earlier in this chapter, but let's look at it a little more closely. It is a legal document that declares our old selves dead and our new selves alive. This covenant defines our relationship with God and gives us a new identity. Because the new covenant is a legal document, it is binding in the courtroom of heaven. So, if the new covenant says we are a saint, a child of God, and an heir, then these are legally binding realities. It also means that a big part of our journey moving forward will involve putting off the old and putting on the new as we learn to live a life worthy of the calling we have received (Eph. 4:1).

If the new covenant establishes the legal foundation of our relationship with God, the next element, the Holy Spirit, serves as our guide to that relationship. You can draw a stick figure bird next to the two arrows and write the word "Spirit" next to the bird.

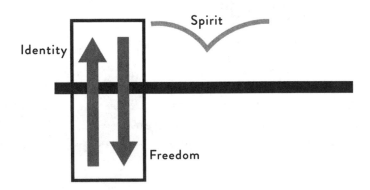

The Holy Spirit brings to life what the new covenant establishes as true. Jesus said we must be born again to enter the kingdom of God (John 3:3–5). He then described what it means to be born again as being "born of the Spirit" (John 3:5–6).[1] When I lead people in a prayer of salvation, I also have them pray to be filled with the Holy Spirit.

The Holy Spirit serves as our guide in at least three ways:

1. **Scripture.** The Holy Spirit inspired the writers, gave us an authoritative book to serve as an anchor to our faith, and now helps us interpret and apply these inspired words.
2. **Believers.** The Holy Spirit guides us by other Christians who speak into our lives and help us stay connected to Him.
3. **Thoughts.** Not every thought that enters our mind is ours. Some come from the enemy to tempt us. Some come from the Holy Spirit to guide us. Part of the discipleship journey is developing the discernment to recognize the Spirit's leading.

As you can see, the first three elements of heart-focused discipleship—freedom, identity, and Spirit—are clearly anchored in the gospel. We never leave these three foundations behind. We build our lives firmly upon them. Together, they form a proven pathway to a vibrant walk with God:

- **Freedom.** We need to keep growing in freedom throughout our walk with God as He puts His finger on lies, sins, and wounds that creep in or remain unresolved.
- **Identity.** Christian maturity can be defined as living out of our new identity even under stress. As we mature, our ability to live like a child of God no matter how we feel will increase.
- **Spirit.** We never outgrow our need to walk in the Spirit. Meditation on God's Word, belonging to a people who keep us on track, and growing our ability to recognize the Holy Spirit's leading are essential to Christian growth.

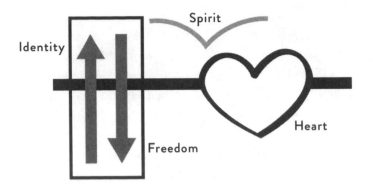

The last element of FISH is called heart focused community. To represent this in the diagram, you draw a heart and write the word "heart" next to it. The reason for distinguishing heart-focused community from some other type of community is to remind us that we need to be in relationship with people who are on a journey of the heart. We need to talk about what is going on in our hearts with them. A heart-focused community is characterized by vulnerability and empathy. It is a place we can correct each other in love. It is a place we can share in safety about our struggles.

> **A heart-focused community is characterized by vulnerability and empathy. It is a place we can share in safety about our struggles.**

I have yet to go to a church that wasn't devoted to community, but that doesn't mean they understand how to create heart-focused community. Too often, small groups serve as the parking lot of the church. Our leaders push to get us connected to a small group Bible study and seem to assume that growth will automatically happen as a result. But most of the people I have talked to have not been very happy with their small group experience. It has not been transformational, and they have not felt like they built strong relationships. There are exceptions, of course, but those exceptions happen when the group actually becomes heart-focused.

FISH AND GO FISH

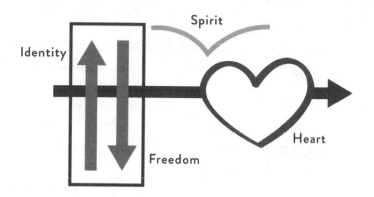

The last element of the fish diagram is to put an arrow on the end of the line of baptism. This arrow represents mission. The idea is that doing life with a group of people who are all growing in freedom, identity, and Spirit-filled living will produce ministry. I look at this in two ways.

First, people growing in their walk with God are more likely to be moved by the Spirit in ways that impact the world around them. Second, people who go into full-time ministry will be more effective if their ministry is anchored in the four elements of FISH. It is no secret that many pastors become isolated and fall into sin. Nor is it a secret that the number one reason most missionaries leave the field is that they can't get along with the other missionaries. How much more effective would our ministries be if they actively pursued the FISH model of heart-focused discipleship?

I was sharing this model with one pastor, and when we got to the last part about mission, he said, "So, what you are telling me is that Christians should FISH and go fish." I laughed. That was pretty good, and that was exactly what I was saying.

Imagine what would happen if you could walk into any church in the world and know that you could find help living in freedom, maturing in your identity, and walking in the Spirit? How would things

If you want a deeper, more vibrant walk with God, you need to pursue growth in all four areas of the FISH model.

change if you belonged to a heart-focused group where vulnerability was met with empathy?

As the diagram above suggests, when the church is working the way it should, there is a constant flow taking place in which people enter the FISH process of heart-focused discipleship and go out from there into fruitful ministry.

You may be thinking to yourself, "I can't find a church like that. Is there any hope for me?" The answer is yes.

Your heart-focused community may not come exclusively from your church. Think about the apostle Paul for a moment. The people who did life with him and shared his trials were not all from one church. He collected "his people" from many churches and many parts of the world. In the same way, in my life, there are people I can share life with at a heart level in my home church, but I also have people scattered around the world who are part of my heart-focused community. The goal here is to understand the path. If you want a deeper, more vibrant walk with God, you need to pursue growth in all four areas of the FISH model.

THE REAL-LIFE STORY OF GEORGE BEBAWI

I had a friend named Dr. George Bebawi who lived a life filled with fascinating and often painful experiences.[2] He was a Jew born in Cairo, Egypt. His mother made him memorize the book of Psalms in Hebrew, but she also made him memorize the Quran in Arabic.

In 1956, when war broke out between Israel and Egypt, he was drafted into the Egyptian military. (An awkward situation for a Jew!) The experience was a disaster. His unit was poorly equipped. They were given guns and ammunition, but it was the wrong ammunition and jammed when fired. When their unit actually faced battle, the officers fled, abandoning the troops. When his unit was finally found, they were arrested for desertion because no one believed their story that the officers were the ones who had deserted. They were all sentenced to execution by firing squad.

The soldiers were stripped down to their underwear and had dots painted on their foreheads as targets for the executioners. They then had to sit all night in a school gymnasium, awaiting their fate.

The soldier sitting next to my friend was a Christian. He said, "Let's pray."

George did not want to pray. He didn't see the point.

So, the Christian issued him a challenge. "Let us pray to Jesus. If he rescues us, you must agree to go to church with me."

Figuring he had nothing to lose, George agreed. In the middle of the night, something shocking happened. President Nassar showed up at the school and asked what was happening. Not wanting to execute so many men, he pardoned them all. George was suddenly free.

Soon after that, he went to a Coptic monastery with the other soldier. When he arrived, the abbot greeted him by name even though they had never met. The abbot proceeded to tell him intimate details about his childhood that no one else knew—not even his family.

"God has been talking to me about you," he told George.

A few weeks later, George converted and began studying to become a Coptic priest. He later earned a PhD and became an internationally respected scholar.

After these accounts, the story gets even more interesting, if you can believe it!

George wrote a long letter to the new Egyptian president, Anwar Sadat. It made such an impression on the president that he invited George to become one of his advisors. When Sadat made peace with Israel, it was George who wrote the speech he delivered to the Israeli government.

Later, Sadat was assassinated by Islamic radicals. George was supposed to be in the car with him that day, which initially led to suspicions that he was part of the plot. However, George was a Christian, and the assassins were radical Muslims. It was soon obvious he had nothing to do with it.

In fact, the same people wanted George dead also. Eventually, he was poisoned. It happened just before he got on an airplane to visit a university in Europe. By the time the plane landed, he was so weak he had to be rushed straight to the hospital.

At the hospital, he had a vision. He saw Jesus walking toward him wearing brightly colored robes. He was quoting the end of Mark 16 in Arabic until he said, "You shall drink deadly poison, and it shall not harm you at all" (Mark 16:18). He then kissed George on both cheeks, and he woke up to discover that the doctors had already signed his death certificate. As he later confided to me, "Being raised from the dead will change your life, let me tell you!"

George had a dramatic life. But his transformation followed the FISH pattern perfectly.

Freedom

While at Cambridge, George spent hundreds of hours in therapy and sessions with prayer ministers as he sought freedom from an enormous amount of trauma in his life that included imprisonment and torture. Without the freedom he gained by dealing with these root issues, he would have been stuck, and we would never have met.

Identity

George had a well-anchored sense of his identity in Christ. Once, while sitting on a park bench in Indiana, someone noticed he was from another culture and asked, "Where are you from?" His quick answer was one simple word, "Heaven." They looked puzzled, so he followed that by saying, "I am the son of God!" He said it for the shock value and to get their attention. But he went on to share his story of why an Egyptian Jew chose Christ and what it meant to be a child of God. He later told me that his real heart passion was evangelism.

Spirit

From the earliest days of his life as a Christian, George was mentored in Spirit-filled living. The abbot in his monastery taught him to practice listening prayer. The abbot encouraged this practice by telling George that whenever he came across a passage of Scripture he did not understand, he was to stay in his room, pray, and listen until God made the meaning clear. Then he was to come and speak to the abbot.

Having been schooled in conversational prayer, George learned to pay attention to God's leading in his life. In fact, the reason he was not in the car with Sadat on the day he was assassinated was that the Holy Spirit had told him not to go. His life had been saved because he had become familiar enough with the voice of God to obey that prompting.

Heart-Focused Community

When I first met George, he was teaching at a Baptist church in Indianapolis. George was an intellectual. He taught Semitics at Cambridge University. He spoke and studied in numerous languages. I once visited his house only to find him wearing his Cambridge robes with a half dozen books in different languages spread out on his coffee table. He said, "Please excuse me. I was born in the wrong century."

Despite his impressive education, George's passion was not academics. His passion was the body of Christ. He invited me to join a group that met in his home twice a month. There were students from the local Catholic university, Eastern Orthodox priests, Lutheran ministers, Baptist pastors, and more. It was quite the mix.

He said, "Muslim factions hate each other, but when they are threatened by a common enemy, they unite. Christians don't do that. We don't take care of each other. We say, 'It is only the Catholics who are in trouble, or it is only the charismatics.' We don't love each other the way Christ told us to."

He did everything he could to build a Christian community in which iron sharpened iron. He didn't want to form a new denomination or even get everyone to agree. He wanted to see the body of Christ learn to love each other well.

YOUR JOURNEY TO TRANSFORMATION

The goal of heart-focused discipleship or FISH is to help people in their transformation journey. Your life story may not be as dramatic as George's was, but no matter what experiences, questions, or wounds you have, your transformation can follow the FISH pattern too.

God, in Christ, has laid an amazing foundation for us. Now we need to learn how to build on it well.

In the remainder of this book, I want to introduce you to practical tools you can use on your journey. I want to be your guide on a path of transformation as you learn how to experience freedom, understand your identity, live in the Spirit (which includes learning to think scripturally), and prioritize building relationships with people who are also on a journey of the heart. God, in Christ, has laid an amazing foundation for us. Now we need to learn how to build on it well.

CHAPTER 4

DEALING WITH THE WOUNDS OF THE PAST

WHILE ON STAFF AT A CHURCH early in my ministry, I got into a conversation with a seminary student who attended the church. He had been active in campus ministry and had personally discipled dozens of young adults. However, the young professional he was meeting with at the time wasn't making any progress.

"I've tried everything," my classmate said, "but even though he has a medical degree and is very smart, he can't seem to follow the simplest line of reasoning when it comes to the Bible."

Then he looked at me and remembered my dad taught spiritual warfare at the seminary. He knew I had helped many people with demonic issues, and suddenly a light went on. "I've tried everything except spiritual warfare," he said. "What would you do?"

I suggested that he slip a single line into their opening prayer the next time he met this man. That line was: "In the name of Jesus, I bind any demons from interfering with what we do here today."

I didn't think much of the conversation until the following Sunday, when my friend came to me and exclaimed, "You are never going to believe what happened!" I gave him my full attention, and he continued. "I prayed to bind demons as you said, and for the first time, he understood everything we discussed. He didn't glaze over as he had at other meetings. I also found out that he had a secret sin he had never shared with anyone and that he had grown up in a family that practiced witchcraft."

That explained a lot. It was no wonder this poor fellow was getting demonic interference as he tried to study the Bible. My friend then asked, "What do I do now?"

That was a great question. The sad part was that I didn't know of a single church in the area that could have helped him. I suggested they read Neil T. Anderson's book *The Bondage Breaker* and that he walk this person through the Steps to Freedom in Christ explained in the book.

These steps were a tool I had used many times, and they impact people's lives greatly. They walk people through identifying and renouncing root issues that give the enemy permission to a place in their lives. Dr. Anderson first developed them as a seminary professor at Talbot. He was tired of seeing so many graduates go into ministry with clear areas of spiritual bondage unaddressed.[1] The steps address seven foundational issues that often ensnare people:

1. Counterfeit spirituality (the occult)
2. Deception (lies we believe)
3. Bitterness
4. Pride
5. Rebellion
6. Habitual sins (compulsive behaviors, addictions, etc.)
7. Ancestral sins[2]

A few weeks later, I saw my classmate again. They had started going through the steps, and his friend was making significant progress. However, in the process, my fellow seminary student realized he needed the same kind of help.

He had strongholds in his own life that needed to be torn down. He asked if we could meet together, so we made an appointment for later in the week. Going through the Steps to Freedom in Christ was helpful, but it also uncovered many other issues that were going to need more attention. If I had known then what I know now, I would have helped him start a heart-focused community with some of the people he was discipling so they could launch their journey together.

My friend's experience is not an isolated story. My dad once told of a seminary student with a temper problem who came to him for help. He had a pretty wife and two adorable kids. He was a good student with a lot of ministry experience on his résumé. The chances were high that he would interview well and become the pastor at a church when he graduated. But there was, of course, this anger issue.

When things weren't "apple pie neat" at home (to use my dad's term), he would fly into a rage. The morning he came to see my dad, he had thrown a phone across the room and left his little ones crying in fear as it exploded against the wall. His wife had called to make the appointment with a veiled threat to her husband that she wouldn't put up with this much longer.

As my dad met with this man, it was clear that he had gone as far as traditional

Freedom is not simply a counseling or recovery issue. It is fundamental to discipleship.

discipleship could take him. No one in his life had ever treated freedom like it was part of the discipleship process. It hadn't even come up. He was about to graduate and go into full-time ministry, and he was still in bondage to what you might call a "rage compulsion." Can you imagine the damage that was awaiting the church that hired him?

As my dad met with him that morning, my dad asked, "Is there any chance that you have another area of your life that feels out of control?" The young man hung his head in shame and confessed to a pornography addiction. That day he started a journey to freedom. My dad helped him identify and remove demons related to these compulsions and taught him about his identity in Christ (something that had not been taught in seminary). Things changed dramatically after that, and several years later, he reported that while he had the usual struggles most people have, the compulsions were gone.

Reflecting on this experience reminds me of how important freedom is to the discipleship process. Imagine how different your walk with God would be if someone helped you tear down the strongholds that kept you stuck? Too often, the church has relegated this type of activity to counseling centers, recovery ministries, and the like. Yet freedom is not simply a counseling or recovery issue. It is fundamental to discipleship.

ROCKS AND ROPES

Dean Vander Mey runs Set Free Ministries in Grand Rapids. For decades, he and his team have trained people to help others experience freedom in Christ. They have met with thousands of people stuck in areas related to the occult, false religion, bitterness, fear, rage, addiction, and more. I asked Dean to speak at one of our conferences, and he told me a story I have never forgotten. I think you will see why.

Dean traveled to a village in Africa, and one afternoon, he spread the word that there would be a special event that included a race. The winner would earn five dollars. At that time, five dollars would buy rice for a week in most rural villages.

A few hours later, people started to gather, and Dean asked, "Who is the best athlete in the village?" Everyone knew the answer to that. They all pointed to the fastest runner. He wagged his head and smiled as he sheepishly admitted that he was the fastest. Dean asked him to participate. Then, looking around the audience, he invited a young girl to join the race. Everyone laughed. There was no way a little girl could beat their champion.

However, there were a few special rules Dean had not yet revealed. First, he pulled out a backpack and asked the man to wear it. Then he invited some of his friends to find the heaviest rocks they could find and fill up the backpack. Again, people laughed at the sight of the athlete getting weighed down with rocks. The race was starting to look a little more even. Next, Dean pulled out a rope. He asked a couple of the athlete's friends if they would mind binding his legs together. They were all smiles as they bound up their friend's feet with the rope.

Now it was time for the race. At this point, the girl could have skipped to the finish line and won the race. The fastest runner in the village wasn't going anywhere in a hurry.

Once they finished the race, Dean rewarded both participants for helping. He then opened his Bible and read, "Therefore, since we are surrounded by so great a cloud of witnesses, let us also lay aside every weight, and sin which clings so closely, and let us run with endurance the race that is set before us" (Heb. 12:1).

If we are going to run the race of the Christian life, we need to get free from the lies we believe and the sin that enslaves us.

He then explained that no one can run the race of the Christian life if they are in bondage to the rocks that weigh them down and the ropes that ensnare them. The rocks are like the wounds from our past that cause us to believe lies, and the ropes are like the sin that enslaves us. If we are going to run the race, we need to get free from both. All heart-focused discipleship must address these issues.

DEALING WITH ROCKS

A common problem that keeps us stuck and in bondage is unresolved pain from our past. Wounds from the past create fertile soil for the devil's lies, and lies create bondage. Thus, Jesus could say, "the truth will set you free" (John 8:32). Dean employed the imagery of rocks to represent both wounds and the lies they produce. I often use rocks also to symbolize the baggage we carry with us from our past. That baggage can weigh us down, so we feel more like we are crawling on the path of life than running a race.

In my book *Understanding the Wounded Heart*, I introduce a simple model to help people understand how even small wounds can create fertile soil for the lies of the devil and how our flesh makes vows that form the strongholds we face. I call this model WLVS: The Demonic Radio Network—Broadcasting All Deception, All the Time. WLVS stands for wounds, lies, vows, and strongholds.

The WLVS model is a warfare model. It includes the world, the devil, and the flesh. The world wounds us. The devil lies to us. The flesh makes vows. The result are strongholds that keep us enslaved. It works like this.

Wounds

When our hearts get wounded, it is like someone takes a plow and digs a furrow in the soil of our hearts. The freshly plowed ground is ready to receive seeds.

Lies

On either side of the fresh wound stand two farmers. One is the devil. He is the father of lies (John 8:44) and has a bag full of "lie seeds." The other is the Holy Spirit. He is the Spirit of truth (John 16:13) and has a bag full of "truth seeds." In our pain, it is often easy to hear the enemy's voice whispering his lies, especially if we are still children or are not in an intimate walk with God at the time. The devil's lies interpret our pain. He tells us that God has abandoned us and cannot be trusted. He tells us that we are worthless and alone. He tells us lies that feel true because of the pain we have experienced.

Vows

If the devil succeeds in planting his lies in the wounded places in our hearts, our flesh believes those lies and begins to make vows of self-protection. A vow is usually an "I will" statement. Here are a few examples:

- I will never trust God with my heart again.
- I will never trust men again.

- I will never trust women again.
- I will prove to my dad that I am worthy of love.
- I will prove to my friends that I am cool.
- I will never let anyone close enough to cause me pain.

Vows are like vines growing from the seeds that get planted in the wounded places in our hearts. If a wound has taught me to believe that I am unlovable, and I vow never to let anyone close enough to find out how bad I am, that will give shape to my life and create a stronghold that keeps me in bondage.

Strongholds

Eventually, fruit starts to grow on the vine. It is usually unwanted fruit like anger, addiction, fear, depression, and shame. It is the fruit that generally sends us to therapy for help. The problem I see is that too much modern mental health focuses on symptoms rather than roots. They do what I call "fruit picking." It looks like this:

- Do you have an anger problem? Here are five things you can do to manage your anger.
- Do you have fear? Here is some medication, and maybe you should take a yoga class.
- Do you have depression? Here is some medication and five steps for managing your depression.

Now, don't get me wrong. I am all for managing symptoms. I would rather see people manage their anger than let it run amok. However, wouldn't it be better to get to the root issues that are causing all the problems at some point? That is what WLVS is all about. It is a model for helping us get at the root causes of our baggage.

Strongholds also keep us separated from God. If you are a sheep and a roaring lion wants to eat you for lunch, what is your best defense? Is it to become a super sheep and take down the lion on your own? No.

Your best protection is to stay as close to the shepherd as possible. The lion knows this, so his goal is to get you away from the shepherd, where you are easier to handle.

Since the lion is also the father of lies, his primary strategy is deception. He wants to plant lies in the wounded places in our hearts that cause us to avoid the shepherd. He either wants us to believe lies about the shepherd or lies about ourselves. He wants us to think the shepherd is not as trustworthy as people say he is or fill us with so much shame that we believe the shepherd doesn't want to bother with us. He wants to put a rift between God and us. This is why so many of the devil's lies focus on the way we see God and ourselves.

Years ago, I read the book *The Hidden Rift with God*.[3] Its basic premise is that most Christians secretly don't trust God. Most of us are angry with Him about something. The problem is made worse because most of us feel the need to hide our anger at God. After all, good Christians aren't angry with God (or so we think), and we want to be good Christians.

> **God would rather we be honest with Him about how we feel than hide it.**

I learned a long time ago that God would rather we be honest with Him about how we feel than hide it. I was in a group that was working with a woman who had been ritually tortured in childhood on numerous occasions. She had major trust issues with God. In fact, she hated Him. After working together for a while, she took her first step toward a relationship with God by praying this way:

> God, you know I hate you. My whole life, I have blamed you for everything that happened to me. But these people seem to think you are okay, and they seem to be okay, so I am willing to give you a chance.[4]

Clearly, this was not a prayer of total and complete surrender to the will of God, but it was the beginning of a journey that led to enormous transformation. Since then, I have often told people, "God will only meet you at the point of your honesty, not on the basis of your performance."

STRATEGIES FOR HEALING

In my book *Understanding the Wounded Heart*, I explain the WLVS model more fully. I also explain four core strategies for recovery. Here is a brief introduction to these strategies.[5]

1. Build Joy

One of the most important habits we can cultivate is to build joy by practicing appreciation. The Bible consistently reminds us to praise the Lord and give thanks in all things. There is a subset of Psalms that even begin, "Give thanks to the LORD, for he is good" (Ps. 106:1; 107:1; 118:1; 136:1). And Psalm 100:1–5 provides a classic example of a call to enter God's presence with appreciation and praise:

> Make a joyful noise to the LORD, all the earth!
>   Serve the LORD with gladness!
>   Come into his presence with singing!
> Know that the LORD, he is God!
>   It is he who made us, and we are his;
>   we are his people, and the sheep of his pasture.
> Enter his gates with thanksgiving,
>   and his courts with praise!
>   Give thanks to him; bless his name!
> For the LORD is good;
>   his steadfast love endures forever,
>   and his faithfulness to all generations.

The idea behind building joy is to grow our capacity to live with gratitude even when times are hard. Getting your brain in a state of appreciation for five minutes just two or three times each day can make a significant difference in your outlook on life. When I say a state of appreciation, I mean thinking about something that makes you smile and letting yourself dwell in that feeling for five whole minutes. Most of us can think of things that make us smile, but we don't stay there for more than a few seconds.

For example, how often have you looked at a beautiful sunset and thought, "Wow, that is amazing!" only to turn your attention back to your problems within a few seconds. Imagine if you set up a chair, got yourself some tea, and enjoyed watching the sunset for five minutes. But this is only one way to grow the practice of appreciation and build joy. You might scroll through family pictures on your phone or make lists of some of your favorite experiences. Doing things like this two to three times a day teaches your brain that gratitude and appreciation are normal and helps to build your capacity to find some joy every day.

2. Forgive

When we are dealing with root wounds that have given ground to the lies and vows in our lives, it makes sense that forgiveness would play a major role in our recovery. Forgiveness is sometimes used synonymously with emotional healing as if forgiving someone cures all the pain and fixes the problems created by the wound. However, healing and forgiveness are not the same thing. In some ways, forgiveness is a business transaction.

Forgiveness is renouncing our right to collect on that debt and handing it over to God.

The most common metaphor for forgiveness in the New Testament is canceling a debt. The idea is that when people wrong us, they owe us a debt. Forgiveness is renouncing our right to collect on that debt and handing it over to God. I often think of it as handing the problem over to the kingdom of God collection agency. When we choose to forgive someone, we remove the enemy's legal claim on us. It is a choice we make so that we can be free—not from the emotions of bitterness because that sometimes takes time—but from the adversary's claims.

One of the most remarkable examples of forgiveness I have witnessed involved a young woman with schizophrenia. I met her at a speaking engagement and asked when her problems started. She had a very specific answer: she had been gang-raped when she was fifteen. It had happened just around the corner from where we were meeting. That is a profound evil.

As we continued the conversation, I said, "I assume you have been through a lot of therapy for this." She nodded. Then I asked, "Have any of your counselors ever walked you through forgiving the men who did this?" She said no and went on to say, "They actually told me that I don't need to forgive them because what they did was so bad."

I thought about that for a moment and replied, "It is certainly true that they don't deserve your forgiveness. But if you thought Jesus wanted you to forgive them out of obedience to Him, would you be willing to do it?" She said yes, and we walked through a simple prayer acknowledging the pain they had caused and choosing to forgive them in the name of Jesus.

Nothing dramatic happened that I could see. The young woman didn't even have a lot of emotion about it. However, when I came back to that church the following week, she met me at the door and asked, "Can I share my testimony?"

That caught me off guard, but I asked, "What is it?"

She said, "Ever since we prayed last week, the voices in my head have stopped. Also, on Monday, I told the dark shadowy figure that has been following me around that he had to leave, and it is gone, too." I said, "Sure, you can share that story!"

To be clear: I am not saying her schizophrenia was gone. I am saying that she experienced freedom from two forms of oppression that didn't need to be present in her life, and forgiveness was the key that unlocked her chains.

3. *Take Thoughts Captive*

Perhaps the most powerful force the enemy exerts in our lives is deception. The lies the enemy tells us often don't feel like lies. They feel true. Thus, we don't feel like we are being deceived. For example, instead of asking, "What lies did you start to believe after you were wounded?" I often ask people this question, "What started feeling true after this wound happened?" Here are some common responses:

- I am all alone in this world.
- No one cares about me.
- God is cruel.
- God doesn't love me.
- I am a slut.
- If anybody knew what happened, they would be disgusted with me.
- If my own mother hates me, how could anyone love me?

Four Strategies for

EMOTIONAL HEALING

Build Joy

Forgive

Take Thoughts Captive

Listening Prayer

An important strategy in the battle for the mind is taking thoughts captive. Paul originally applied this term to evangelism (2 Cor. 10:5). He was entering into cultures dominated by worldviews that were hostile to the gospel and tearing down strongholds and argumentations that set themselves against Christ and His kingdom. However, by extension, the term applies to any situation in which we battle with the kingdom of darkness over beliefs.

My father often told the story of meeting with a missionary who had a problem that was more common than he thought. Whenever he would listen to praise music or try to worship at church, his mind would start to fill with pornographic images.

My dad asked him the obvious question, "Are you filling your mind with these images throughout the week?"

"Absolutely not," he answered, "I hate that stuff. I used to have a problem with it many years ago, but I avoid it carefully now."

My dad replied, "If you are not putting those thoughts in your head, and God is not putting those thoughts in your head, where do you think they are coming from?"

The missionary began to understand that these thoughts were attacks from the enemy that were going unresisted. My dad advised him to simply command the devil to leave the next time this happened and see what difference it made.

About a year later, the missionary met with my dad before heading back to the field. He said, "Thank you so much for teaching me about taking my thoughts captive. Not only did the pornographic attacks in church stop, but it has also changed my marriage and my ministry. I had no idea how often the enemy was planting unwanted thoughts in my head, then accusing me for having them."

> **We all need to understand the basic principle that not every thought that enters your head is yours.**

From time to time, my wife has awakened with a feeling of dread. As soon as she started dealing with this as a spiritual attack, it stopped. We all need to understand the basic principle that not every thought that enters your head is yours. Some come from the Holy Spirit prompting you to do good. Others come from the enemy to tempt you. This is not always a direct temptation to sin. It often comes as a picture, an emotion, a random thought, or a familiar thought. Learning to recognize thoughts that tempt us to adopt a negative emotion, attitude, or behavior and resist those thoughts is a fundamental part of the discipleship process.

As I was writing this section, I got the following text from a friend.

She overheard her five-year-old using his loudest, meanest voice to say, "Bad thoughts, go away right now in Jesus' name! You are not welcome here! And if you don't leave, I'm gonna call on the Lord, and He's going to smash you to smithers."[6] Now that is what I call taking thoughts captive!

4. Listening Prayer

Several years ago, I was invited to teach on emotional healing to the staff of a crisis pregnancy ministry in Ukraine. After teaching them the WLVS model, we talked about how to help people connect with Jesus in their painful memories. Afterward, one of the translators asked if I would meet with her and pray about some painful memories in her past. My wife and I agreed. We followed a model I teach in *Understanding the Wounded Heart* called REAL prayer. It works something like this:

R. Father, help me to **REMEMBER** whatever memory You want to heal. We did this with our translator and God reminded her of a memory of abuse that happened in her kitchen as a child.

E. Father, **EXPLORE** this memory with me. What do I need to remember about it? As my wife and I did this with the translator, she remembered the deep emotions that were stirred and could describe in detail what the kitchen looked like and what people were wearing.

A. Father, I **ASK** you to do whatever you need to do to heal this memory. She repeated this prayer then closed her eyes and paid attention to what came to her mind.

L. **LISTEN.** At this point we asked the translator to revisit the memory in her mind and see if anything was different. We asked if anything felt different or if she had any new thoughts. She did. As she looked around, she felt the Lord's presence with her and the pain of the memory began to fade. She felt peace. We encouraged her to see if the Lord wanted to do something more, and she found herself experiencing the Lord's presence in such a vivid way, she felt like years of stress were being washed away. From the outside looking on, my wife and I could see her physical body begin to relax.[7]

As we wrapped up that night, all sorts of Scripture came to life for our new friend. She had known these verses all her life, but after sensing the Lord's presence she realized just how true it was that God had never left her or forsaken her (Deut. 31:8) and how true it is that He is close to the brokenhearted (Ps. 34:18).

As you can see from this story, I wasn't really in charge of what was happening. I wasn't suggesting what she should remember or what she should visualize. We were just pressing into the situation and testing for counterfeits. Only Jesus can heal. I can't heal anyone. People can't heal themselves. When we talk about healing memories, we are talking about helping people connect with Jesus in such a way that He heals the pain of the past. And one way we know she really met with Jesus is the fruit of the experience. She experienced real healing. She found it easier to trust Jesus when we were done. She felt peace she didn't have before.

Today, there are many ministries that teach approaches to this type of emotional healing process. There are also New Age counterfeits of this type of ministry, which is why testing is important. Not everything that happens in the name of Jesus is from Jesus. If you want to read an interesting account of counterfeit religious experiences, you might try Johanna Michaelsen's book *The Beautiful Side of Evil.*[8]

TREMENDOUS LIFE CHANGE

These four strategies for emotional healing can bring tremendous life change. Joy helps us build the capacity to handle hardship. Taking thoughts captive tears down the bars of deception that drive negative emotions. Forgiveness sets us free from bondage to bitterness and the unwanted consequences that flow from it. Listening prayer allows God to minister directly to us, involving Him in the process and making a level of healing possible that cannot come in any other way.

Now that we have introduced the idea of removing the rocks that weigh us down so that we can run the race set before us with greater freedom, in the next chapter, we will look at how to untie the ropes that entangle us and keep us stuck.

CHAPTER 5

FREEDOM THROUGH SPIRITUAL WARFARE

ONE OF THE MOST DRAMATIC life transformations I ever witnessed involved a man named Mark.

Mark was a tough character. He stood about 6'5" and weighed around 300 pounds. He had a quick temper and was one of the most intimidating people I knew.

The first time I met Mark was after preaching one Sunday. He marched down to the front of the church like a man on a mission. He walked up to me and said, "Preacher, I just want to make one thing clear. I am only here for my wife. I don't want you calling on me. I don't want you asking me to volunteer. Just leave me alone. Do we understand each other?"

I don't remember exactly how I responded, but I was thinking, "Whatever you say. Just don't hurt me."

After an introduction like that, you can imagine my surprise when Mark called a few days later. He was sobbing.

"I'm in a hotel room," he said. "My wife kicked me out. Is there any chance we can get together and talk? I've got to get my life together."

I cleared out several hours that week and met with this broken man. It turned out that Mark had survived a rough childhood. His father had been abusively cruel, but there was more. Older kids in his neighborhood had bullied him. Mark grew isolated and angry. At one point, he said, "I've never told anyone this before, but some of the older kids sexually abused me." Whenever someone tells you something they have never told anyone else, you need to take that seriously.

Together, we walked through the WLVS model and the REAL prayer process taught in the last chapter. His recollection of one memory was extremely graphic, and the emotions were raw. But when he asked Jesus to do whatever needed to be done to heal that memory, he experienced a dramatic connection with Jesus in a way he had never dreamed possible. The resolution of the pain and the new perspective he received changed everything he had believed about Jesus. After that, the thought of giving his life to Christ was a no-brainer.

We used the rest of the week to start Mark's discipleship journey. We began with freedom and spiritual warfare. I led him through the renunciation of past occult activity. Next, he repented of some of his more habitual sins, and we evicted wicked spirits that had taken advantage of both these things to take up residence in his life. He chose to forgive his father and the kids who had bullied and abused him. After helping Mark get free from some of these strongholds, I helped him understand his new identity in Christ and some basics of how to walk in the Spirit. By the end of the week, Mark was a changed man. He didn't become perfect, but the change was obvious, and he became a gentle giant.

A few weeks later, I had the privilege of walking him and his wife through some counseling and, shortly after that, they renewed their wedding vows. He started a Bible study with two other men in the church on Thursday mornings at 6:30 a.m. He developed a passion for helping teenage boys who were falling through the cracks. He took them under his wing and became like an uncle or a second father to some of them.

One of my dreams is that people like Mark will be able to walk into any church in the world and get help. It's my desire that churches and mature Christians will teach them how to get free from the ropes, as I mentioned in the last chapter, that keep them in bondage. How amazing would it be if every church had a freedom ministry with people capable of being spiritual parents to those who need to grow, were devoted to heart-focused discipleship, and developed a clear pathway to freedom and maturity? It could change everything.

As you pursue your journey to greater freedom and maturity, you will need to understand how spiritual warfare works. Sadly, this is no longer common knowledge. However, it has been part of Christian ministry from the very beginning. Deliverance from demonic spirits was such a standard part of Christian culture during the Roman Empire that one bishop, an apologist named Tertullian, was able to claim that everywhere the Christians went, they drove out demons.[1] He made this claim like it was a common practice and everyone knew it.

THE REALITY OF DEMONS

We live in a world that often treats demons like metaphors. When we say that people "battle their demons," we mean that they struggle with tormenting thoughts and behavioral compulsions without any concept that there are actual entities called demons. But one young lady, who thought she was battling metaphorical demons, found out just how real they were.

This woman had been hospitalized several times for an eating disorder. Since a common abbreviation for an eating disorder is E.D., she was taught in therapy to call her eating disorder "Ed." They taught her to treat Ed like a person she needed to learn to live with. The problem was that sometimes, Ed woke this girl up in the middle of the night and screamed

> We live in a world that often treats demons like metaphors without any concept that demons are actual entities.

at her. He constantly told her she was worthless and pathetic. As you can imagine, Ed was tough to live with.

Then, one day, she had a freedom appointment with a friend of mine who was a very experienced spiritual warfare prayer minister. He helped her evict "Ed," who turned out to be a literal demon. In a moment, her life changed.

Before I continue this story, let me take a moment to walk you through what typically happens at a freedom appointment. In most cases, two people get together with a prayer partner for support. They normally use a tool like Neil T. Anderson's *The Steps to Freedom in Christ* that helps them identify root issues that permit demons to impact their life. As issues arise, those seeking freedom usually repent of sin, forgive specific people who have wronged them, or renounce lies that have been blinding them. They then cancel the permission these root issues have given to the enemy and command him to leave. (These are all actions I'll describe in greater detail for you later in this chapter.)

Depending on how many layers of issues a person needs to resolve, these sessions can last as little as fifteen minutes or turn into many sessions over several years. When the process goes on for years, it doesn't mean the person is bad or not doing things right. It means there are usually lots of layers—often a lot of childhood trauma—and there are normally a lot of non-warfare issues that need to be addressed. Spiritual warfare is not a silver bullet that fixes everything quickly. On Deeper Walk International's website, you can find information about tools and resources for training people to run freedom appointments.

Now back to the story of this young lady. Several weeks after she found freedom from her eating disorder, she wrote:

> Basically, ED THERAPY teaches you how to live with [the disorder]. It teaches you ways to cope with it and make it quieter, but I never heard that I had the authority to make it leave me. It never was a part of me. It was a demon terrorizing and bullying me [and] I have the

power in the name of Jesus to send it back to where it came from. That's the only way you can have complete freedom.[2]

She is now thriving and is in the process of becoming a certified therapist. And while demons do not cause all eating disorders, the point is that demons are real, and when demons create our problems, the only solution that will work is spiritual warfare.

HOW SPIRITUAL WARFARE WORKS

In its most basic sense, spiritual warfare is about taking ground back from the enemy. Ultimately, this involves evangelism and reclaiming people groups from the principalities and powers that oversee them. All evangelism—and especially missions—is a spiritual warfare activity. It is a breach of territory long held by the kingdom of darkness. The kingdom of light invades the kingdom of darkness, and the dark powers are not happy about it. This invasion is the primary reason we often hear stories of power encounters in missionary contexts. When the apostle Paul wrote about spiritual warfare, he was most commonly writing with a missions mindset.

For our purposes, we want to focus on the issue of recovering ground from the enemy at an individual level. When people live in bondage to the adversary, they need to reclaim surrendered ground. We need to understand two principles to comprehend how this works: *permission* and *authority*.

Authority

The believer's authority is rooted in the idea that we are seated with Christ in the heavenly realms (Eph. 2:6). To be seated with Christ is to be in a place above demonic powers (Eph. 1:19–23). It puts us in a position of spiritual authority.

Our authority is real, but as with police officers, there are limits to that authority. If I am driving down the street and a patrol car flashes its lights at me, I will pull over to the side of the road because officers have the right to do that under law. However, if the officer says, "Your shirt doesn't match your pants, go home and change," well, he doesn't have the authority to make me do that. At that point, he is crossing the line established by the law. But if he says, "You were driving ten miles per hour over the speed limit, I'm giving you a ticket," the law does give him the authority to do that.

Authority is the right to represent power. When an officer pulls me over, I don't wait to see who it is before complying. I don't say to myself, "You know, if it's Sue, I'll stop. But if it's Bob, I'm out of here." As long as the person has the right to represent the power of the government, I am not just dealing with Bob or Sue. I am dealing with the entire legal system. In the same way, any Christian who confronts a demon is in a position of authority. We represent the kingdom of God, and thus we can speak "in the name of Jesus," just as a police officer can address us "in the name of the law."

One woman came to see me because she suspected demonic activity in her life. She told me it began when she visited a church that did not teach a biblical worldview. This particular church denied the inerrancy of Scripture, the virgin birth, and the resurrection of Jesus. And, when she told them she was struggling with anxiety and depression and needed help, they sent her to a yoga class that was meeting in the church. However, this wasn't a Christianized yoga class which might be defensible (though I would still advise against it). This class was a full Hindu session led by a guru.

As she sat in the circle and followed the instructions, the guru touched her forehead. What happened next shocked her. She felt energy pulsate from the spot where he had touched her, fill her body, concentrate at the base of her spine, and then refocus in the center of her forehead. From that point on, she became psychic.

She wondered if it might be the Holy Spirit since she was a Bible-believing Christian. She asked me if she had been given the gift of prophecy because, from that point on, she didn't need caller ID. She knew who was calling before she looked at the phone, and she was never wrong. It was the same with people knocking on the door of her apartment. She always knew who was there before she opened the door. I had heard of such things before and assured her this was not the Holy Spirit. Instead, it was something called a Kundalini spirit that impersonates the Holy Spirit.

As we walked through a prayer process together, she renounced her involvement with yoga and the access she had given demons by participating in this religious ritual. I then encouraged her to command the demons to leave, but she hesitated.

"Are you sure I can do that?" she asked. "Shouldn't I just ask Jesus to do it for me?"

"No," I explained. "Jesus won't do for you what He has given you the authority to do for yourself." I then showed her the following diagram:

The crowned heart at the top represents God, who is love and is sovereign. He is the only God and is above all else. Beneath Him are stars. These stars represent the angels. One is upside down and darkened to represent fallen angels or demonic powers. Beneath the stars are humans. They are depicted as hearts because they are made in the image of God and are designed to share a love relationship with Him. The human with the crown is the Christian.

After showing her this diagram, I drew an arrow from the Christian to the spot next to God. I explained that Christians are seated with Christ above the angels and demons (Eph. 2:6), which puts us in a position of both victory and authority. Therefore, when Christians address demons, we are speaking down to them. They are not equals. They are not above us. They may be stronger and smarter than us, but we have the authority to represent the power of God's kingdom. Demons know that if they mess with us, they are messing with the kingdom of God. The question is whether or not we know it. Too many Christians live as victims because they do not understand what it means to be victors in Christ.

> **Too many Christians live as victims because they do not understand what it means to be victors in Christ.**

The woman understood, so she took a deep breath and commanded the spirits to leave and take all their "gifts" with them. She immediately felt lighter. A year later, she told me her psychic abilities had ended, and so had her depression. She was walking more closely with God than ever.

Permission

In the courtroom of heaven, God is king. Therefore, demons can only do what they have permission to do. In this present evil age, they can roam the earth and tempt people. However, as we see in the book of Job and in Satan's request to sift Peter like wheat (Job 1:6–12; Luke 22:31), if they want to do more than that, they need additional permission.

As with Job and Peter, sometimes God grants consent to test someone. Permission does not indicate that God agrees that what is happening is good. Instead, it means that He will not intervene to stop what is occurring. For example, if a demon were to stand before the court and say, "I have a right to torment this person because of what they have done," the demon may be correct. God does not keep people from being tormented simply because He doesn't want to see anyone in pain. There are rules to the way the universe operates.

Other times, demons are summoned and sent on missions by people who practice the occult. For example, a witch doctor cursed a missionary to kill him. On his way to the shaman's village, this missionary nearly died when his bicycle burst into flames unexpectedly. However, when the missionary arrived at the village safely, the witch doctor—seeing that Christ's power was greater than his—converted.[3] In the Bible, we see the idea of demonic activity in response to human petition when the sorcerers of Egypt were able to turn their staffs into serpents (Ex. 7:11). Scripture forbids this type of sorcery (Ex. 22:18; Deut. 18:10).

However, most of the time, permission is given directly by our behavior. We offer the devil a place in our lives when we sin and do not deal with it quickly (Eph. 4:26–27). Often, we do not realize we are giving permission to the enemy. We may have no idea that demons are involved, but we don't have to know what we are doing for spirits to take advantage of us. One of my colleagues grew up in a Christian family that did not understand spiritual warfare. His parents bought him a Ouija board for Christmas. Even though he was a Christian, he gave demons permission to harass him by using it. He didn't recognize what was happening until years later when he renounced what he had done.

We also permit demons to torment and deceive us when we enter into *agreements* with them. How do we enter into agreements with demons? If a wicked spirit tempts me to believe his lie rather than God's truth, and I do, it is as if I am shaking hands with him and saying, "You are right. God is wrong. I'll look at this your way." It is the same with attitudes and actions. If I agree to do things the enemy's way, I am entering into an agreement with him that gives him greater access to my life.

It sometimes helps me to think of demons as birds. Imagine a young man is walking down the street, and on the corner, there is a tree full of birds. These birds are hunters, but they don't attack directly. They are the kind of hunters who set traps.[4] These birds set traps by using bait to lure us into their snares. We call this temptation. One of the reasons demons do this is that they like to enslave people. They relish the role of master. Whereas God wants children who trust Him and obey Him, demons want slaves to control.

As the young man walks down the street, suppose an attractive girl crosses the road in front of him. It is no big deal if he has trained himself to live with a pure heart. He may notice that she is attractive, but it ends there. If he has not trained himself to be pure, his fleshly desires can lead him to fixate on her and start heading down the path of lust.

At this point, demons will not stay out of the picture. Recognizing what is going on, one of the birds who is particularly good at tempting people with lust might fly over and begin to whisper ideas into the young man's ear. If he does not resist the temptation, he essentially enters into an agreement with the demon that says, "Okay, I'll do this your way." He has given the demon permission to stick around. The demon doesn't necessarily enter the young man, but the evil creature isn't going to leave, either. It will stay close by and use every opportunity to increase its power over the young man.

The situation doesn't usually end there. Once a person gives permission to one demon, others start showing up. Another bird might fly over and whisper thoughts of shame to the young man: "I thought you were a Christian. You are such a pervert! What a rotten person you are."

Again, if he does not resist the enemy, he will enter into another agreement, and suddenly another demon starts hanging around. Perhaps another bird comes and whispers thoughts of fear: "You better hope no one ever finds out what you are really like. You will be exposed. You will be discredited. You could lose everything." Before this bird can finish, the first one reminds him just how good it would feel to indulge his lust, and a cycle is born.

If the young man treats all of these thoughts as if they are simply his flesh and never takes a stand against the enemy, he can find himself living with a flock of these despicable creatures following him around wherever he goes. He may not be possessed, but he is not free.

TESTING

One of the ways we distinguish problems that originate in the flesh from problems that originate because of demons is through testing. We are told to resist the devil and make him flee (James 4:7). You can't do that with the flesh. It doesn't submit to authority, so you can't make it flee. For example, I have had anxious thoughts that came from the enemy and anxious thoughts that were simply from my flesh. I tried resisting the devil and commanding him to flee in both cases. When it is the flesh, it doesn't resolve anything. But when it is the devil, I have often experienced immediate relief. That is a form of testing. There are also times when it can be both. If my flesh has already started the process of giving in to fear, demons aren't going to stand back and watch. They are going to try to make things worse. Sometimes, I need to resist the devil *and* renew my mind in order to overcome a temptation.

Through the years I have met with countless people who were in bondage to sexual sin, fear, anger, despair, and all sorts of other problems. They had tried for so long to get free that most of them felt a level of hopelessness that there was no solution for their bondage. This sense of hopelessness was especially true when the only solutions offered by the church were to spend more time reading the Bible or to make an even stronger commitment to break the habit. Most people who give such advice have no idea how powerful a demonic compulsion can be or how overwhelming and relentless the attack is.

THE THREE CS: CONFESS, CANCEL, COMMAND

At the individual level, spiritual warfare includes resisting temptation, taking thoughts captive, and, when necessary, breaking agreements we have made with the enemy. We can do this through what Karl Payne calls the three C approach to gaining freedom from demons:

C—Confess. Admit that you have sinned and entered into an agreement with the enemy.

C—Cancel. Break your agreement and ask Jesus to cancel the permission any demon has to stick around.

C—Command. In the name of Jesus, command the demons to leave and take all of their works and effects with them.[5]

The battle gets much easier when you don't have a flock of demon birds harassing you all day long. One man who battled pornography went through an intensive program to help him break his habit. The program helped, but he confided in me that he felt like a dry drunk. He avoided specific websites, but his taste for porn had not gone away. However, his mind cleared up once he dealt with the issue as a warfare problem and went through the three Cs. He didn't have the same compulsion toward fantasy. His battle wasn't over, but with the demons gone, he only had to lift his shield of faith and stop an arrow here and there. Before, it was like this constant barrage of arrows he couldn't possibly hope to deflect.

We have added a fourth C—*Commit*—to the three Cs Dr. Payne uses. The fourth C is simply a reminder that once you are done evicting a demonic spirit, it is important to commit that area of your life to the lordship of Christ. This might be done with a prayer like this, "Father, I commit this area of my life to you and surrender it to the lordship of Christ. Please fill any vacated places in my life with your Holy Spirit."

Four Steps for

EVICTING DEMONS

Confess

Cancel

Command

Commit

SPIRITUAL WARFARE AND THE BODY

It is instructive that in the gospel of Mark, half of the miracles of healing performed by Jesus involved casting out a demon. It is because demons can do more than harass our thought life and drive us crazy with their constant attacks. They can also affect our bodies.

Once you are done evicting a demonic spirit, it is important to commit that area of your life to the lordship of Christ.

For example, I have a friend who met with a woman who had suffered terrible headaches for nearly a decade. She had gone to the best medical clinics in the country and tried the latest medicines and dietary treatments, but all to no effect. After years of pain, someone suggested that the issue could be related to spiritual warfare. This thought led her to contact my friend.

As he interviewed her, he asked a couple of obvious questions: When did this start? And did anything out of the ordinary happen to you about that time? She had answered these questions before, but my friend listened with a kingdom worldview and picked up on something the medical community had missed.

This lady's headaches started when she came home from a missionary trip to Peru. While she was there, she visited Machu Picchu. To remember the occasion, she bought a souvenir. It was a replica of a knife like the kind used in pagan rituals to cut the hearts out of sacrificial victims. Does anyone see a problem here? My friend did. He led her to destroy the knife and cut off any demonic connection related to it. He helped her do this and reports that her headaches stopped the moment she threw the knife into the fire and commanded the demons to leave. A chronic issue that had no medical solution was resolved instantly.

This story reminds us that when we have a spiritual warfare problem, only a spiritual warfare solution will resolve it. I could share numerous stories in which strange medical issues were resolved when spiritual warfare issues were addressed. These instances don't mean that all strange medical issues are demonic. But it does make me wonder why spiritual warfare is so often the last thing we try.

SOUL-L: HOW WE SURRENDER GROUND TO THE ENEMY

There are many ways we can surrender ground to the enemy and give demons permission to affect our lives. To keep it simple, I like to summarize some of the most common ways we open doors to the enemy with the acronym SOUL-L (as in, "I am in a battle for my soul"). SOUL-L stands for sin, occult, unforgiveness, lies we believe, and lineage.

Sin

We don't get a demon every time we sin. However, if we do not confess our sin, we permit demons to have a place in our lives (Eph. 4:26–27). If we justify our sin or deny that we have sinned, demons don't sit back and say, "Well, they are in enough trouble. I think I'll stay out of it." They are like sharks. When they smell blood in the water, they attack. Unconfessed sin is like an open door that invites demons to enter our lives. Here are some common ways we open doors to the enemy through sin:

- **Rebellion.** Rebellion often grows out of bitterness. It is the spirit or attitude that wants to do anything except what we are told to do. In 1 Samuel 15:23, it is compared to divination, which is an occult practice that seeks spiritual knowledge apart from God. Just as divination (a form of witchcraft) can let demons into your life, so can rebellion.
- **Pride.** Pride is the spirit that exalts itself above others. Pride makes us want to sit at the seat of honor and have others greet us as someone of importance (Luke 11:43). Healthy pride refers to the satisfaction of a job well done. Unhealthy pride takes pleasure in being better than others.

- **Compulsive sin.** When a demon came upon King Saul, he was overcome by a compulsion to kill David. This overwhelming desire happened twice with David (1 Sam. 18:11; 19:10) and once with King Saul's son, Jonathan (1 Sam. 20:33). Compulsions to do things that violate God's will are often a sign of demonic activity.

- **Idolatry.** Worshiping actual idols is still a major problem in the world. Paul wrote that Christians engaged in idolatrous activity had "fellowship" with demons (1 Cor. 10:20–21). Not only does literal idolatry surrender ground to demons, but an idol can also be anything or anyone we worship as a savior. Thus, Paul could say that greed was idolatry (Col. 3:5), because greed looks to money to deliver us from our problems.

- **Lust/sexual immorality.** One of the traits of early Christianity was its complete intolerance of sexual immorality. As Paul wrote, "But among you there must not be even a hint of sexual immorality" (Eph. 5:3 NIV). His words do not mean we are not allowed to struggle with lust. They communicate that we are not to hide our struggles or deny they are a problem. We seek help.

- **Deception.** When we lie to ourselves, we justify our sin. When we lie to others, if we are doing it to get away with something wrong or to get an innocent person in trouble, God calls it an abomination (Deut. 25:16). However, when people lie to show mercy to someone in danger, the Bible commends it. For example, Rahab lied about the spies she hid (Josh. 2:4–5) and was commended for her faith (Heb. 11:31). In the same way, people who hid Jews from the Nazis and lied about it were not guilty of sin.

There are other sins not listed here that also open doors to the enemy. But these specific ones have been listed to spur our thinking as we ask God to show us if we have opened any doors to wicked spirits in our lives. It is a good idea to periodically examine ourselves to see if

It is a good idea to periodically examine ourselves to see if we have let sin get a foothold in our lives. If we have, confess it to God and to someone with the maturity to deal with it.

we have let sin get a foothold. If we have, confess it to God and to someone with the maturity to deal with it.

Occult

The occult is a specific kind of sin in which we participate directly with demons. Occult activity can be divided into two sorts—the pursuit of spiritual knowledge from a source other than the true God and the pursuit of spiritual power from an alternative source. Here are some common examples of these two types of occult activity:

- Secret knowledge
  - Astrology and horoscopes (seeking knowledge and guidance from the stars)[6]
  - Fortune tellers (seeking knowledge and guidance from the spirit realm)
  - Divination (reading omens and seeking information from the spirit world—Ouija boards, tarot cards, etc.)
  - Necromancy and séances (seeking to contact the dead)
  - Spirit guides (spiritual beings who speak to us)

- Secret power
  - Spells and incantations (using words to summon spiritual power)
  - Rituals (sacrifices, ceremonies, and pacts made with/for spirits other than God)
  - Curses (using words to summon spirits to harm others)
  - Astral projection (the power to travel in the spiritual realm)
  - Sorcery (mastery of the occult arts)

All such activity is forbidden by Scripture (Deut. 18). It is seeking knowledge and power from spirits other than God. If sin opens a door to demons in our lives, the occult invites them in and asks them to be friends.

Early in my ministry, a family asked me to meet with their grown daughter. She had been diagnosed with schizophrenia because she heard voices.

I suspected these voices might be demons and that the occult may have played a role in opening the door to them. I asked if she had ever been involved with the occult, and she said no. Then I showed her a list like the one above, and she still said she had not participated in any of them. Finally, I went through the list one by one and explained each one.

By the time we were done, she had confessed to regularly participating in over twenty occult activities.

Not only that, but she had lived with her boyfriend and had sexual sin on top of the occult issues. To make it worse, her ex-boyfriend turned out to be a warlock who had put a curse on her when they broke up.

One by one, we closed each of these open doors and evicted the demons that had been permitted to enter. By the time we were done, her mind was quiet, and she didn't hear voices anymore.

> **Five Common Ways**
> **We Give Demons**
> **PERMISSION**
>
> **Sin**
> **Occult**
> **Unforgiveness**
> **Lies we believe**
> **Lineage**

We live in an occult-saturated world. When I was a kid, witches were portrayed as spooky and scary. Most of them were green and had giant warts. Today, witches are seen as cool and sexy. The stigma has been almost completely removed and, in many cases, reversed.

Unforgiveness

Another specific sin that gives ground to the enemy is unforgiveness stemming from bitterness. As we talked about in the last chapter, the Bible often describes forgiveness in terms of debt. When someone wounds us or wrongs us, they owe us a debt. Forgiveness is canceling that debt. At the root of many of our issues, we often find unforgiveness. If we do not forgive those who wrong us, it opens the door to all sorts of other problems.

At the root of many of our issues, we often find unforgiveness.

At the beginning of this chapter, I wrote about working with Mark. As you might suspect, he needed to forgive many people in his life. His first instinct was to think that he wasn't ready to forgive them. What he meant was that he didn't *feel* any forgiveness for them.

However, I asked him to approach the process like a business transaction in which he chose to cancel the debt they owed him. Taking this approach, he decided to forgive his dad, the neighborhood bullies, and several others who had wounded him in his life. Once he chose to forgive, he commanded any demons who had taken advantage of his bitterness to leave. I could see his body visibly relax as he did this.

We wrapped up this part of the session by praying two more things. First, Mark prayed that God would bless these people by bringing healing and redemption to their lives. Next, he asked God to take responsibility for the debt owed him. The prayer went something like this, "I hereby transfer this debt to the kingdom of God collection agency. If there is any debt left to be paid, I agree that it is God's to collect, not mine."

Not only did Mark forgive those who had wounded him, but he also forgave himself for the poor choices he had made and renounced the bitterness he had toward God for allowing all of the bad stuff that had happened in his life.

Second, we cannot forgive our own sins. What we are actually doing when we say, "I choose to forgive myself," is accepting God's forgiveness.

Today, when I pray with people, I usually use the more theologically accurate words. But for years, we prayed to forgive God and ourselves. God honored the prayers, and demons were made to leave.

For example, after speaking on spiritual warfare at a Christian college, a young lady asked to talk to me. She had been tormented with guilt after having sex with her boyfriend before they married. Since getting married, she had been plagued with nightmares. She said, "I have asked God to forgive me a thousand times, but nothing ever seems to change."

Can you tell what was missing in her experience? If she asked God to forgive her a thousand times, what was she not doing? She was not *receiving* that forgiveness.

I led her in a simple prayer to forgive herself and receive God's forgiveness and command any wicked spirits that had been tormenting her to leave. A year later, I was in the same city for a wedding, and this young lady was there. She pulled me aside to let me know that she had not had another nightmare since praying to forgive herself.

LIES WE BELIEVE

Satan is the father of lies (John 8:44). So, it makes sense that one of the primary ways he enslaves people is through deception.

It helps me to think of deception as an illusionist's trick. Professional magicians go to great lengths to hide reality so that we only perceive what they want us to see. The deception happens because we only observe part of the picture. It may look like the magician just made his assistant disappear. All of the facts seem to support this conclusion because any details revealing what is really going on are expertly hidden.

In the same way, the devil is a master illusionist. He gets us to see only what he wants us to perceive. As a result, we believe the lie he is selling. What makes deception effective is that the facts we rehearse in our minds seem to be true. Indeed, many of the facts are accurate. Thus, we don't see where the deception is.

The devil's lies work like propaganda. They establish a narrative that drives our emotions. For example, when President Woodrow Wilson determined that America needed to join England as an ally in World War I, he had a problem. Most Americans didn't want to join the war. Polls showed the country divided nearly evenly as to which side we should join if we entered the conflict.

To rally people to support joining England's cause, President Wilson started a Department of Propaganda headed by his campaign manager.[7] The manager promptly changed the organization's name because it doesn't help to tell people you are the Department of Propaganda. He was so successful in demonizing the Germans that by the time America entered the war, polls showed that 90 percent of Americans favored siding with England.

The American people became angry enough to support war with Germany for one primary reason: the narrative had changed. They had come to view Germany as evil. Their emotions and behavior changed because what they believed had changed. The new story altered people's feelings (hatred and anger), which changed how they behaved (full support for the war effort). It even became dangerous for people to let others know if they had doubts about the legitimacy of the war or sympathy for the German cause.

Just as President Wilson's propaganda team led America into war, so the devil's propaganda team leads us into bondage. To combat the devil's strategy of deception, it is important for us to learn how to practice discernment. One of the tools I use to do this is a simple two-part prayer asking God for clarity. Part one is, "Father, would you show me in words or pictures how the devil wants me to see this person or this situation?" Part two is, "Please show me in words or pictures how you want me to see this person or situation."

When I led marriage retreats more regularly, I always had couples pray this as one of their exercises. It was very common for people to report significant improvement in their marriages once they discerned the devil's role in distorting how they saw their spouse. One man started to cry during our last session as he confessed the mental picture of his wife. He had seen her as almost a clown with very few redeeming qualities. God had corrected his view of his wife and, in the process, led him to repentance. Learning to see her through God's eyes renewed his love for her and taught him to take his thoughts captive quickly, so he didn't go back down the dark hole that had been dug by the enemy.

LINEAGE

Part of dying to the old self (Rom. 6:6–7) involves putting off all associations with generational sin. The idea of generational sin is new to some Christians, but it is a common theme in the Bible. The law of Moses, for example, banned Ammonites and Moabites from entering "the assembly of the LORD" for ten generations (Deut. 23:3–6). Jesus said the blood of all the prophets that had been shed since the beginning of the world would be punished in His generation (Luke 11:50–51). That proved true when the Romans first destroyed the temple in AD 70—killing tens of thousands of people in the process—and then destroyed the nation itself during the Bar Kochba Revolt around AD 135. The point here is that the Bible is familiar with the idea that sin can create consequences for future generations, and that is what I mean when I say that lineage can open the door to demonic activity.

A young professional who made his living as a scientist made an appointment to see me because he had been battling panic attacks and fear for several years, and the problem was getting worse. The young man was a devout Christian. He had been reading a lot of Christian books to increase his faith. He figured the best solution to fear was more faith. That made sense, but it wasn't working.

As I listened to his story, I thought about permission and authority. I wanted to know if demons were driving his fear. If so, I wondered what was giving them permission to do it. We prayed together and asked God to remind him of the very first time he experienced fear. He remembered being alone at home as a child when—in his own words—something invisible jumped on him. He screamed out in fear and experienced his first real panic.

The experience sounded like a demonic attack to me. So, the question was: What would have permitted a demon to do something like that to a child? The most likely answer was that it was something done by the adults in the house. Since the attack was related to fear, I asked if any other family members struggled with fear. He didn't have to think long and replied, "My mother and her mother are the biggest worriers I have ever met." That made sense. They had given permission to demons to be present in their own lives, and those demons were trying to stake a claim in the next generation. They were tempting the young boy hoping to ensnare him in the same trap they had used successfully on his ancestors.

That day, in my office, he prayed to renounce whatever he had done to permit demons of fear to be in his life. He then renounced whatever permission they had through his family line. As he got halfway through the prayer, he got stuck. Specifically, he could not finish the word, Jesus. He was trying to command ancestral demons to leave but couldn't say the name of Jesus. I stepped in, bound the demons from interfering, and he finished the prayer.

Our job is to put off everything that keeps us tied to that old life or the kingdom of darkness and to put on Christ.

You could see his demeanor change. "Wow!" he said, "I would never have dreamed my lineage had anything to do with my issues. I come from a good, Christian family." A few years later, I met him again, and he told me he had not had a panic attack since dealing with the ancestral demons that day.

Another story that has stuck with me through the years tells of a man in Southeast Asia whose family had been the caretakers of a pagan shrine for many generations. The young man attended an evangelistic crusade and gave his life to Jesus. When he returned home, he sensed the war between the powers of his old gods and his new God. He knew he could not serve two masters. So, he walked up to the shrine and announced, "I have found a new God. He is more powerful than you.

I choose Him and will no longer serve you." Then he tore down the shrine, set it on fire, and, for good measure, urinated on it. Now that's what I call making a break with generational sin!

THE REST OF MARK'S STORY

I opened this chapter talking about Mark. He quickly became one of my best friends. But sadly, my relationship with him only lasted five years. I got a call one night from his wife. This time she was in tears. Mark had died of an apparent heart attack.

I'll never forget the funeral. Hundreds of people packed the church and person after person testified to some act of kindness or some way in which Mark had made their lives better. One confused young man only knew the old Mark. He had not spent time with him after his conversion and life change. He stood up and said, "I don't know who you guys are talking about. When I knew Mark, he was the scariest person I had ever met. But it sounds like he found religion or something, and I am really glad to hear that."

Knowing what Mark's life had been like before coming to Christ and diving into heart-focused discipleship, I couldn't help but imagine how different his funeral would have been if he had died just a few years sooner. Reflecting on his life reminds me how amazing God's grace really is and how dramatic transformation can really be.

Freedom is an essential element of the discipleship process. It is hard to run the race set before us when we are in bondage. We need to untie the ropes that entangle us and keep us stuck. Our job as those who have died with Christ is to put off everything that keeps us tied to that old life or the kingdom of darkness and to put on Christ.

In the next two chapters we are going to look at the primary foundation on which a vibrant walk with God is built. We will explore our new identity in Christ and why the devil works so hard to destroy this crucial foundation of the faith.

CHAPTER 6

IDENTITY IN CHRIST

IMAGINE YOU ARE AN ORPHAN living in the streets of London in the early 1800s. You belong to a group of people who are the outcasts of society. You are at home among them and have learned to fit into that group. Your values and lifestyle have been shaped by your sense of belonging and your day-to-day experience of living as an orphan in poverty.

You are occasionally in trouble with the law because part of your survival skills includes petty theft. One day, you hear a rumor that the king has issued a decree granting a pardon to all orphans. You simply need to go to the local court of law and claim it. Being wise to the ways of the world, you think this might be a trap. But soon you meet a few orphans who show you their legal certificate of pardon. The police are no longer after them. It has really worked. So, you also go to the local court and get a pardon.

Here is a question to consider: Would receiving a pardon for your bad behavior be any incentive to change the way you live? Would you be motivated not to steal in the future? Maybe so, but maybe not. After all, this simply means you can't get in trouble for it anymore. This issue is part of the problem with traditional discipleship. It often reduces the gospel to the offer of a pardon for sin. In the words of Bob George in *Classic Christianity*, traditional discipleship has "neglected half of the gospel"—namely, our identity in Christ.[1]

Now imagine that one day the king comes to your neighborhood. He arrives in a carriage surrounded by soldiers on horseback. To your surprise, some of them start calling your name. People point you out, and soon you realize you are being taken to see the king himself. You may wonder if you are in trouble. Perhaps the pardon wasn't real after all. But as you enter the carriage and glance toward the king, you realize he is happy to see you.

The king welcomes you warmly, invites you to sit with him, and begins to speak. "I want you to know that I am sorry you have had to live as an orphan all these years. I knew your parents," he says. "They were good people."

You are not sure where this is going, but it sounds promising.

He continues, "I have had all of the paperwork drawn up, and I want you to know that I have adopted you as my son."

With that, a servant hands him a parchment. He shows it to you. They are your adoption papers. Suddenly, you find out you are a child of the king. You don't know the king at all, but suddenly you find yourself bonded to him in a very personal way.

He tells you, "This means you are in my will. You will receive an inheritance of land and other valuables at the coronation of my son. He is off fighting a war right now, but when he returns, I am handing the kingdom to him. You will receive your inheritance then. While the war is going on, you will not live in the palace, but I will supply everything you need. You can make your requests as my child, and they will be handled accordingly."

He then extends to you a choice, explaining, "If you accept this offer, I will expect you to represent our family well and work for the good of the kingdom. It will not be easy. Many people hate our family and hate our kingdom. By identifying with us, you too will become the object of scorn to many. Some of your close friends may reject you. Life will not get easier. However, when my son returns, and the war is won, an account will be made. If you do well, your inheritance will be all the larger." He finishes by saying, "I know you don't know me intimately yet, but I am hoping you will come to trust me. I am giving you all of this because I love you just as I loved your parents. What do you say? Are you willing to accept my offer?"

Saying yes is an act of faith. It is a decision with a lot of consequences. But in the end, it is a no-brainer. You sign your name to the parchment, and suddenly you find yourself a prince who is no longer an orphan.

Now let's ask the same question as before: Would being adopted as a child of the king be any incentive to change the way you live? Absolutely. Your change of identity would alter who your people are, what is important to you, what is good and evil, and how you think of yourself. It would all transform even if it didn't feel real at first. This change is reflected in Paul's words, "Therefore, if anyone is in Christ, he is a new creation. The old has passed away; behold, the new has come" (2 Cor. 5:17).

Next, imagine it's a few weeks later, and you are walking along feeling great about life and still basking in the wonder of the transformation that has occurred. But out of the shadows comes a voice. "Who do you think you are kidding?" it whispers. "You are no prince. I know who you really are. I know what you are really like."

It is a moment of temptation. You could agree with the voice in the shadows and begin to doubt your new identity. If you do agree with it, you start noticing it seems to show up more often, reminding you of your flaws and what is really true about you. Soon, you stop acting like a child of the king. You go back to your old lifestyle. It is possible to be royalty and yet live like a pauper.

But what if, instead of agreeing with the voice in the shadows, you called it out. What if you said, "You there. Step out here where I can see you. Oh, I recognize you. You are a liar and deceiver. You are right about one thing. I was all of the bad things you said, and sometimes I still mess

God has given us a new identity in Christ. It is legally and eternally true.

up. But I am a child of the king, and if you talk to me like that again, I'll call the palace guard and see what they have to say about this."

Just like the king in this story gives the orphan a new identity, God has given us a new identity in Christ. It is legally true. It is eternally true. It is meant to be the foundation of a whole new approach to life. Let's take a deeper dive into this new identity and how being raised with Christ has changed everything.

JUST LIKE MEPHIBOSHETH

In the Old Testament, we read the story of a rather obscure character named Mephibosheth.[2] He was the grandson of King Saul and the son of David's best friend, Jonathan, and had become crippled when he was dropped as a child (2 Sam. 4:4).

Even though Mephibosheth was Jonathan's son, King David did not know him. They had never met. Mephibosheth had not performed some remarkable feat or done a tremendous service to the king. In fact, in many cultures, David might have been expected to have Mephibosheth killed because he was a direct descendant of the former king and thus a potential rival.

Instead, David did the opposite. He lavished Mephibosheth with gifts. He brought him into the royal palace and treated him like a member of his own family. He also gave him King Saul's estate as an inheritance (2 Sam. 9:9). It was shocking to see the extent of the blessing David showered on a man he didn't know. So, why did David do this, and why does it matter to us?

Everything David did for Mephibosheth was done out of love for the young man's father, Jonathan (2 Sam. 9:1). The two friends had entered into a most unusual covenant (1 Sam. 20:1–17; 23:15–18). Jonathan was the crown prince and the expected heir to the throne. However, the prophet Samuel had anointed David to be the next king. That created a very awkward situation. Normally, Jonathan and David would have been rivals. Instead, Jonathan accepted the Lord's verdict. He entered a covenant with David in which he agreed that his friend would become king instead of him. He told David, "You shall be king over Israel, and I shall be next to you" (1 Sam. 23:17).

Jonathan's one request was that if anything happened to him, David would be kind to his family (1 Sam. 20:14–15). They entered into a covenant to confirm this. David's lavish blessing to Mephibosheth was not due to anything Mephibosheth had done. It was not a reward for good behavior or valor in battle. It was a free gift based on a covenant. Does that sound familiar?

This story is instructive because it illustrates God's grace to us through Christ. Just as Mephibosheth did nothing to earn the blessings he was given, so we do nothing to earn the gifts that God gives us in Christ. God blesses us because we are connected to His beloved Son. Just as David blessed Mephibosheth lavishly because of Jonathan, so God has blessed us lavishly because of Christ.

EVERY SPIRITUAL BLESSING

In Ephesians 1:3, the apostle Paul wrote, "Blessed be the God and Father of our Lord Jesus Christ, who has blessed us in Christ with every spiritual blessing in the heavenly places." It is the opening concept in a long burst of praise that ends in verse 14. Let's unpack this passage briefly.

- **"Blessed be the God and Father of our Lord Jesus Christ who has blessed us . . ."** To bless is to do or say what is good for someone. We bless God because He blessed us. And when we do, we state what is good about Him and honor Him with what is good.
- **". . . in Christ . . ."** The term "in Christ" is used often by the apostle Paul. Every time I read "in Christ" in Paul's letters, I think, "new covenant." If something is true of us in Christ, it

is legally true of us under the new covenant. Baptism is the ceremony that celebrates our entrance into the new covenant. It symbolizes our death to the old and resurrection with Christ to a new reality in which we are bonded to Jesus, under the new covenant, and born of the Spirit. Before dying with Christ, I was "in Adam" (1 Cor. 15:22). Being in Adam meant I was subject to the curses and judgments pronounced on all the descendants of Adam. After rising with Christ, I am "in Christ," and I am the beneficiary of all the blessings that come from being bonded to Him both through the new covenant and the Holy Spirit.

- "   with every spiritual blessing   ." As a result, we have been given "every spiritual blessing," and those blessings are granted and guaranteed by the new covenant. Notice further that the blessings we gain are spiritual. In this life, we do not yet receive all of the physical blessings God has for us. We still get sick. We still have frail bodies. We still live in a broken world. An age is coming in which we will be blessed with every physical blessing. We will receive new bodies and live on a new earth, but for now, we have received every spiritual blessing. I will have more to say about these in a moment.

- ". . . in the heavenly places." The term "heavenly places" refers to the courtroom of heaven, or what is sometimes called "the divine council" (Ps. 82:1). We get a few glimpses of God's courtroom in Scripture (1 Kings 22; Rev. 4–5). In these scenes, we see God enthroned as king. His throne is surrounded and sometimes transported by heavenly creatures called cherubim. They are fearsome creatures and protectors of God's glory. Around God's throne are other thrones. This throne room represents the decision-making center of the universe. God's divine council passes judgment on issues concerning the human race. It is the ultimate courtroom of the universe. It is where God issues decrees and passes judgment.

In the next several verses of Ephesians 1, Paul introduced many of the spiritual blessings that are ours in Christ:

- We have been chosen (1:4).
- We have been adopted according to God's eternal plan (1:5–6).
- We have been redeemed and forgiven by His lavish grace (1:7–8).
- We have been granted an eternal inheritance (1:11–12).
- We have been sealed with the Holy Spirit (1:13–14).

These are all spiritual blessings that are legally ours under the new covenant. No wonder Paul was so excited. Through no merit of our own, God has lavished upon all who believe more blessings than we could have ever dreamed. Paul also knew there was more to come. God's eternal plan includes an amazing inheritance. It is this inheritance—"this hope"—that serves as an "anchor of the soul" (Heb. 6:19).

At the heart of Paul's outburst of praise is the idea that God had an eternal plan to create a family from all the nations of the world and unite that earthly family with His heavenly family. Jesus is the point of connection for everyone, uniting everything in heaven and on earth together under His leadership.

Despite the best efforts of the kingdom of darkness, God's plans are guaranteed. Everything He ever wanted for us is ours in Christ.

In keeping with this plan, God predestined all of the blessings listed above to belong to those of us who are in Christ. It was always in His heart and mind to redeem us and make us part of His family. To accomplish this, He waged war against the principalities and powers that rebelled against Him. He defeated them at the cross and will destroy all of their works completely when Christ returns. Thus, despite the best efforts of the kingdom of darkness, God's plans are guaranteed. Everything He ever wanted for us is ours in Christ.

LEGAL ISSUES

Whenever we read that something is true of us "in Christ," we can think of that as a blessing granted to us in the new covenant. In this sense, "in Christ" statements are like legal clauses in the new covenant. They give us pardon, adoption, citizenship, and sainthood in Christ and have binding authority in the courtroom of heaven.

We can picture it this way. Imagine that you walk into God's courtroom on judgment day. The book of your deeds is opened, and you are called to account for what you have done with your time on earth. Do you want the court to use the covenant of law   as given to Moses in the Old Testament—as the basis for judging you, or do you want them to use the new covenant, also known as the covenant of grace? If the court used the law, we would all be found guilty. The only thing the law can do is condemn us for our sin. Grace cleanses and forgives us.

Sometimes I imagine Moses taking one of the stone tablets on which the Ten Commandments were written and dragging it along the ground, thus drawing a line in the sand. That is what the law does. It draws a line in the sand. That line is good. There is nothing wrong with it because God's law is perfect. However, once I cross that line in the sand, the only thing the law can do is condemn me. When it comes to judgment day, I do not want to be under the law. I want to be under grace.

In Christ, I am under grace and governed by the new covenant. My deeds are judged according to a completely different system than the one created by the law. Building on an analogy Paul used in 1 Corinthians 3:10–15, we can think of our experience on judgment day as crossing a river of fire. Christ is our barge. We are ferried across the river on Him, and we are safe because He is our foundation.

Next to us on the barge are all the deeds we have done in this life. The good deeds are like gold, silver, and costly stones. They are refined by the fire of the river and become even more valuable. Our worthless deeds are like wood, hay, and stubble. They are easily consumed by the fire.

Because Christ is our barge, we safely cross the river of judgment and enter the kingdom. However, the size and quality of our inheritance in the kingdom are determined by what has been burned and what has been purified. Our salvation is not dependent on our good works, but our inheritance is affected by what we do with what we have been given in Christ.

There are many aspects to our new covenant identity, but to keep it simple, I have summarized them under four core blessings. You can remember these blessings with the word PACT. (Hopefully, it is easy to connect the ideas of PACT and covenant.)

- Pardon
- Adoption
- Citizenship
- Title: "Saint"

Just as Mephibosheth was given a new identity and lavish blessings because he was part of the covenant David made with Jonathan, we are given a new identity and lavish blessings because we are included in the new covenant that Christ established. Our new identity is *the* foundation of our new life in Christ. As Paul wrote, "I urge you to live a life worthy of the calling you have received" (Eph. 4:1 NIV). Our calling is our new identity. Thus, Paul was summing up the entire Christian experience as learning to live a life worthy of our new identity in Christ. With this in mind, let's take a closer look at the four core blessings of our new covenant identity.

PARDON

At the heart of the gospel is the idea that Jesus died for sinners—the righteous for the unrighteous (1 Peter 3:18; Matt. 1:21). Christ's death dealt with sin in such a way that once we are united to Him in faith, we share in His righteousness and are no longer sinners in God's sight. This doesn't mean we never sin. It means we are no longer subject to eternal

Four Core Blessings of the

NEW COVENANT

Pardon

Adoption

Citizenship

Title: Saint

judgment for our sin. We have become members of the family and have been pardoned. Let's dive a little deeper.

There is a cluster of words found in the New Testament that relate to how Christ dealt with sin—justification, purification, and redemption. Let's take a closer look at these three important concepts.

1. Justification

Martin Luther made the idea of "justification by faith alone" famous. His study in the book of Romans led him to question the church teachings of his day. He specifically attacked the church's use of indulgences. In Luther's day an *indulgence* was a document that granted entry into heaven for anyone who paid money for it.

A battle erupted over Luther's ideas. Eventually, the pope excommunicated Luther and rejected the idea of justification by faith alone. Luther responded by setting the document on fire. Lines were drawn in the sand, and the church has never been the same. (It is worth noting that many modern Catholics now agree with much of what Luther said and embrace the idea of justification by faith alone.)

So, what is justification by faith? You can think of justification as a coin with two sides: forgiveness and righteousness.

Side One: Forgiveness. Forgiveness means that we are forgiven of our sins—a debt has been satisfied and taken away. You can think of forgiveness as erasing all the red ink in our ledger. Paul put it this way in Colossians 2:13–14: "And you, who were dead in your trespasses and the uncircumcision of your flesh, God made alive together with him, having forgiven us all our trespasses, by canceling the record of debt that stood against us with its legal demands. This he set aside, nailing it to the cross." In other words, the document that recorded all of our sins—all of our debt—was nailed to the cross and taken away. There is no more accusation against us. The legal charge that we are debtors has been removed. That is a profound level of forgiveness.

The document that recorded all of our sins was nailed to the cross and taken away. There is no more accusation against us.

Side Two: Righteousness. The other side of the coin of justification is *righteousness*. The word justification in Greek is *dikaiosune*, and it is a variation of *dikaios*, which is the Greek word for righteous. This side of the coin of justification emphasizes that not only have our sins been forgiven, but the righteousness of Christ has been given to us. This is often called *imputation*.

In Romans 3, Paul argued that there is a righteousness from God that is given as a gift (vv. 24–25). This is not a righteousness we earn by our works. It is a righteousness that is given to us as a gift and received by faith. Paul described this further in Romans 4 where he defended the idea that faith is entered in God's accounts as righteousness. Thus, Abraham believed God and it was credited to him as righteousness (vv. 3–5). In Romans 5, Paul praised God for the justification that gives us righteousness as a free gift (*dorea*).

I look at it like this. Suppose I have a bank account in which sin equals my debt and righteousness equals my assets. In that case, God's forgiveness (side one) wipes out my debt by granting me a pardon for sin, and God's righteousness (side two) deposits Christ's own righteousness into my account. Since Jesus died for the sins of the whole world (1 John 2:2), there is enough righteousness in the account to cover every sin I will ever commit with plenty left over. No matter how much any of us sin, it is a drop in the bucket compared to the sins of the whole world. I emphasize this because many people think they have gone too far to be forgiven. They feel like they have crossed some imaginary line that has disgusted God, so they feel like He says, "You are taking advantage of this arrangement. I'm done with you." These feelings are often exaggerated by the fact that many of these people have never experienced unconditional love from anyone and can't imagine receiving it from God.

On the other hand, knowing that all our sins are covered is not a license to sin. Rather, grace teaches us to say no to godlessness and worldly passions (Titus 2:11–13). We have been set free from sin to live a new life. Why would we go back to sin?

2. Purification

Whereas justification is a legal word, *purification* is a religious word. It is related to temple ceremonies as opposed to a courtroom. The Old Testament concept of worship was about entering sacred space and inter- acting with a sacred God.

For God to meet with us, the space we were in had to be cleansed of all that might make it impure and unfit for His presence. The primary way that unclean things were purified in the ancient world was by being sprinkled with the blood of a clean animal. The author of Hebrews tells us that "under the law almost everything is purified with blood" (Heb. 9:22). All of this may sound foreign to most of us. The whole idea of animal sacrifices can seem barbaric to Western ears. To put this into perspective, in most—if not all—pagan religions, sacred spaces and people also had to be purified with blood. The idea wasn't that someone was immoral and had to be forgiven to be in the presence of the god or goddess. The idea was that someone was contaminated by this world and had to be purified before connecting with the unseen world.

Part of what separates Christianity from all other religions is that ours is the only religion in which the divine being, in our case, Jesus, sheds His blood for our purification. In every other system, we must shed our own blood or the blood of a substitute (usually an animal) to enter the presence of the otherworldly or divine. This is a truly remarkable reversal of the usual order of things. It is a demonstration of God's love for us, and the tremendous sacrifice made by Jesus that He did this for us.

One of the blessings that is ours in Christ and made legally binding in the new covenant is that we have been sprinkled with the blood of Christ and thus made pure. We are now fit to be inhabited by God's Spirit. We have been made clean once and for all. Because of this, when we do sin and "dirty ourselves," it does not undo the work of Christ in making us clean and fit for the Holy Spirit's presence. It does mean that we need to confess our sins so we can live in a state of cleanness and receive the full benefit of living with a clean conscience. One of the benefits of taking the Lord's Supper often is that there is a built-in expectation of confessing one's sins and keeping short accounts with God.

3. Redemption

In this cluster of terms related to our pardon, a third idea is *redemption*. To redeem a person is to buy their freedom. This may be from debt, but is core to the idea of having our freedom purchased so that we are no longer slaves to sin. This was a core idea in the apostle Paul's explanation of the gospel. Christ not only died to forgive us of our sins, He also died to purchase us from the master to whom we were enslaved, namely sin. Thus, Paul wrote that we are no longer slaves of sin (Rom. 6:6), and that we have been bought with a price and are no longer our own (1 Cor. 6:20).

Redemption is often connected to the idea of forgiveness because the same price that took care of our debt and filled our bank account with righteousness purchased our freedom from sin and bought us for Christ so that we are now His. We are now slaves of righteousness (Rom. 6:17–18).

Redemption and the Roman slave system. This word redemption is commonly connected to the slave system in ancient Rome. Most slaves in the ancient world were prisoners of war. When the Roman army conquered a city, many of the soldiers and citizens were sold into slavery. The most heinous form of slavery was to be sold to work in the mines. It was a punishment usually reserved for those who were the most rebellious or dangerous to the empire, but it could also be the fate of anyone who made their master angry. It is estimated that nearly half of the people in the Roman world were slaves. Thus, when Paul wrote about slavery, it was an idea with which everyone was familiar.

When a Roman slave was set free, that was rarely the end of the story. In the United States, one of the great mistakes we made when we ended the institution of slavery was that we did not take steps to guarantee the futures of the newly freed slaves. We basically said, "You are free now. Good luck." In Rome, when a slave was freed, they were often given land and some cash to start their new life. In this sense, they were shown grace by their masters. This grace gave them their freedom and the essentials they needed to make a new start in life. It was expected that, out of gratitude, there would continue to be a relationship of loyalty, but this relationship went two directions. The former slave was expected to be loyal to the former master's interests in the marketplace, and the former master was expected to help the freedman overcome opposition and obstacles to the new life he was starting. If this went well, it was a win-win for both parties:

> The "rules" for what was expected of a patron and a client were not painted on Roman city walls. . . . The rules for the truly foundational institutions of society, like family and patronage, went without being said. Everyone knew what the proper behavior was. A good patron solved the problems of his or her clients: assisting with trade guilds, business disputes, refinancing loans and easing tensions with city elders. . . . The patron did "favors" for his clients who then fell under his circle of influence and protection. In return, the client was expected to be loyal (faithful) and was sometimes asked to do things for the patron.[3]

Just as the Roman system of freeing slaves was superior to the American system, so the grace offered by God is superior to that offered by Rome. In fact, the apostle Paul called God's grace lavish (Eph. 1:8). Not only does Jesus buy our freedom, He gives us everything we need for life and godliness through His great and precious promises (2 Peter 1:3–4).

But the grace of God goes beyond setting us free and giving us an endowment. God adopts us into His family and makes us His heirs. We are given authority, title, status, and security. We become members of the divine, royal family. It would be like a Roman master not just setting a slave free but making that slave his heir. It was a giant leap beyond anything the world had ever seen.

> **God adopts us into His family and makes us His heirs. We are given authority, title, status, and security. We become members of the divine, royal family.**

On top of this, it was not just anyone adopting us former slaves of sin—it was the king of the universe and the Creator of us all demonstrating the depths of His love. It is conceivable that a master could do this for a beloved slave who had performed well, but God did this for His enemies. He did it for people who ignored Him, rebelled against Him, and in some cases hated Him (Rom. 4:5; 5:8). There is no greater love.

ADOPTION

Adoption was a common practice in the Roman world. In the generation before the New Testament was written, Julius Caesar famously adopted Octavian. As Caesar's adopted heir, Octavian instantly became the wealthiest man in Rome and held authority over Caesar's estate after he was assassinated. His adoption made him one of the most powerful men in the world. He used his new identity as Caesar's heir to build his power base and eventually become the "first citizen" of Rome. The Senate granted him the title "Augustus," and he became Rome's first emperor in all but name.

An interesting trait of adoption in Roman culture was that it guaranteed an inheritance. Once someone went through the process of adopting an heir, they could not disinherit that person. A father could disinherit his biological son, but it was impossible to disinherit an adopted son.[4] It was no accident that Paul used adoption imagery to describe our new identity in Christ. To be adopted changed everything. Here are a few ways in which our adoption into the family of God changes our lives.

Access

We have a whole new level of access to God. As part of the family, we can come to Him knowing that we are accepted and loved. As we read in Hebrews 4:16, "Let us then with confidence draw near to the throne of grace, that we may receive mercy and find grace to help in time of need." It is encouraging us as children (clients) to go to our father (patron) with our needs, knowing we will be treated with mercy and provided with the grace we need in the trials we experience.

Acceptance

As an adopted child, we know where we stand with God. We know we are "in." We know we are chosen and that we belong. Many Christians struggle to feel God's acceptance because they think it must be earned. They see their connection to God as something like this:

- **Authority**—God is the final authority, and I must perform adequately in order to earn His acceptance.
- **Accountability**—Because God is the ultimate authority, I live my life knowing I am accountable to Him. Pleasing Him is the highest goal.
- **Affirmation**—If I perform well enough and pass the test, God affirms me as worthy of blessing.
- **Acceptance**—If I am worthy, God will accept me, and I can feel good about my relationship with Him.

In Christ, as one adopted into God's family, this order is actually reversed. I begin as one accepted because of Christ's sacrifice. I am then affirmed for my new identity as God's chosen child. Based on my new identity and acceptance, God holds me accountable to His authority. But my life is lived out of trust in what He has done for me, not fear that my performance will lead to my rejection.

Authority

An adopted heir has the right to represent the family in business matters. We can engage with others in the family name. This is related to the idea that we can pray in the name of Jesus and deal with demons in the name of Jesus. As God's children, we have the right to represent the family and exercise authority in the name of Jesus. Just as Octavian was given the authority to handle Caesar's estate through adoption, so God grants us authority through our adoption as coheirs with Christ.

Inheritance

At the heart of Roman adoption was inheritance. Our adoption under the new covenant also guarantees us an inheritance. That inheritance can grow as we engage in the family business and live for the kingdom. As long as Christ is our foundation and our identity is sealed by the new covenant, our inheritance is guaranteed. It grows as we are faithful stewards of that which God entrusts to us.

CITIZENSHIP

I have several friends who entered the United States as refugees but have since gained their citizenship. They had to go through a legal process, and they were sworn into their new identity as American citizens in a legal ceremony. Just as pardon and adoption are part of our legal identity in Christ, so our citizenship is a legal issue. In Christ—under the new covenant—we have become citizens of the kingdom of heaven. This means we are no longer "of the world" (John 17:16). We are "strangers" here (1 Peter 2:11; Heb. 11:13).

Our citizenship is the foundation of two key changes in how we live. First, as citizens of the kingdom, we are ambassadors of the kingdom (2 Cor. 5:20). We are salt and light (Matt. 5:13–14). We represent the worldview and values of the kingdom of God to those who are of this world. Second, as citizens of the kingdom, we are stewards with an eternal perspective (1 Cor. 4:1–2; 1 Peter 4:10). We no longer live for the rewards and pleasures of this world but for those of the unseen world and the age to come (Heb. 11:25–26).

In Colossians 1:13, Paul wrote that we have been rescued from the realm of darkness and transferred to the kingdom of God's beloved Son. Now that our citizenship has changed, we need to put off everything that bound us to the kingdom of darkness. Experiencing freedom does not happen automatically. We sometimes need to fight to be freed from the realm from which we have been rescued.

> **In Christ, we have become citizens of the kingdom of heaven. We no longer live for the rewards and pleasures of this world but for those of the unseen world and the age to come.**

For example, some missionaries came to a primitive tribe in the Amazon jungle. In fact, *National Geographic* called this tribe the most stone-aged people group left on earth.[5] The head shaman was named Shoefoot. In a video about his life called "I'll Never Go Back," Shoefoot describes the process he went through to become a witch doctor. He used drugs and went through rituals to invite various spirits "into his chest."[6] He developed the ability to recognize where the spirits were in his village and the surrounding area. He knew which ones sometimes helped people and which ones were just mean. When Shoefoot first met the missionaries, he saw something he had never seen before. They each had a bright light shining out of their chest. He later learned that this was the Holy Spirit.

Sometime later, Shoefoot converted and was baptized. He even changed his name to Bautista—"baptized one." The bright light of the Holy Spirit entered his chest. However, he had a problem. The other spirits were still living there. He had given himself to them with powerful oaths and rituals.

The missionaries who had led him to Christ did not understand spiritual warfare. They thought the entrance of the Holy Spirit would automatically drive out any evil spirits. But that is not how it works. A war erupted inside of the shaman. He went out into the jungle for a few days and began renouncing the rituals that had welcomed these spirits. One by one, he commanded them to leave. However, there was one that he could not drive out. This spirit was beautiful and powerful. He was not sure he wanted to get rid of it. There was a struggle, and he found himself submitting to the will of the evil spirit. Finally, Jesus showed up and said, "Enough." The seductive spirit left for good, and Bautista was finally fully free.

This shaman had changed kingdoms. He now belonged to Christ and was filled with the Spirit, but there was still freedom to be won. In a similar way, we are warned not to love the world or the things of the world (1 John 2:15). The world belongs to the devil. He is the prince or ruler of the world (John 12:31). I sometimes think of the world as the devil's mistress. She is seductive and enticing, but it is a trap. She flirts with us and gets us to think she has something good to offer. If we are not careful, we will find ourselves in bed with Satan's girlfriend. That is not going to end well.

As citizens of the kingdom, we need to learn to live in a manner worthy of the calling we have received. This means we cannot be double-minded, as if we can have enough of the world to enjoy its pleasures without getting burned by the experience.

TITLE: SAINTS

As Christians, we are given the title *saint*. The word saint is easily misunderstood because we often have associated it with people who are particularly godly or virtuous. It has become common to say, "I'm no saint." But no Christian can honestly say this. We are all saints. Paul did not address a single letter to "the sinners in the church of such and such city." It wasn't that the Christians there were all virtuous. But being a saint is not something earned. It is an identity that serves as a foundation for virtue.

When it comes to understanding what it means to be a saint, it helps me to think of Old Testament priests. Let's use Aaron as our example. Aaron was not a famously virtuous person. He actually led the nation into sin by making the golden calf that Israel worshiped at Mt. Sinai (Ex. 32:4)—not great credentials for becoming a priest. Aaron was not made sacred because he was without sin.

Instead, when this sinner became a priest, he was sanctified. This meant he was set apart with a new identity. He belonged to God, and whatever belongs to God is holy or sacred. Everything that was dedicated to God as His possession became sacred. This was true of the tabernacle, the vessels in the tabernacle, the gifts dedicated to God, the sacrifices offered to God, and the people who served Him. They were holy because they belonged to a God who was not of this world.

Notice the parallels between the process by which Aaron and his sons were made priests (Lev. 8) and the way Christians are sanctified as God's people in Christ:

- The priest was washed with water (Lev. 8:6). We are baptized with water (Gal. 3:27).
- The priest was dressed with new clothes (Lev. 8:7–9). We are clothed with Christ (Gal. 3:27).
- The priest was anointed with oil (Lev. 8:10). We are anointed with the Spirit (1 John 2:20; Acts 2:17–18).
- The priest was sprinkled with the blood of the sacrifice (Lev. 8:22–25). We are sprinkled with the blood of Christ (Heb. 12:24).
- The priest was commissioned into the work of the tabernacle (Lev. 8:33–36). We are commissioned by Christ into a new priesthood (1 Peter 2:9).

As saints, we have become holy ones. This implies more than we might think. In the Old Testament, the term *holy one* was often used for supernatural beings who inhabited the unseen realm. The idea of holiness had less to do with good behavior and virtue than it did with belonging to the unseen realm. Even pagan gods were considered holy, and their priests and rituals were called sacred. They often had temple prostitutes who were considered "holy."[7] This was clearly not a reference to how virtuous they were. The reason holiness and virtue are connected for Christians is that the God to whom we belong is virtuous. We are not set apart to Baal or Asherah. We are set apart to Yahweh through Jesus Christ. To mirror God's holiness is to mirror His virtue and to bear His name and image in this world.

THE CONNECTION BETWEEN MATURITY AND IDENTITY

Since the goal of the discipleship process is to "present everyone mature in Christ" (Col. 1:28), it is important to spell out the connection between our identity and our maturity. Our identity is something God gives us. We are born with heart values. We are given a legal identity in Christ. Maturity is what we do with our identity. We mature as we learn to live out of the heart Jesus has given us and build on the foundation of our identity in Christ.

While identity and maturity are different, they are related. We can measure maturity in terms of our identity. From this perspective, maturity is the ability to act like yourself even under stress. The more mature we are, the more hardship we can endure and still live from our hearts like the people God knows us to be. The less mature we are, the less it takes for us to act like someone we are not.

It is no wonder that our identity is such a battleground. The devil does not want us to live from our hearts. Nor does he want us building on the foundation of our identity in Christ. One veteran counselor said that in over fifty years of ministry every person who had come to him for help had an identity issue. The vast majority did not understand their identity in Christ, and few were in touch with the heart Jesus had given them.

In this chapter we have focused on the new legal identity that is ours in the new covenant as those who are in Christ. In the next chapter, I want to explore identity from the brain's perspective and take a look at what I call "the other half of identity."

CHAPTER 7

THE OTHER HALF
OF IDENTITY

WHEN I WAS A KID, I loved baseball. I played Little League and was usually one of the top players at the park near where I lived. But partway through one season, I went into a batting slump. Hitting a baseball started to feel really difficult. My dad offered to help, and I thought, "Great, maybe he'll take me to the park for some extra batting practice." Instead, he gave me a cassette tape by a sports psychologist. That was not what I was expecting.

The man on the tape told stories about athletes who improved their game by visualizing themselves performing their tasks perfectly. In one study, a basketball team was divided into two groups. One group shot 100 free throws every day for a week. The other group spent the same amount of time sitting in a chair with their eyes closed, picturing themselves shooting and making free throws. At the end of the week, both groups had improved by the same amount.

Based on this idea, my dad had me sit in a chair and picture myself hitting baseballs. To my surprise, I couldn't do it. Even in my imagination,

I would lose my balance, hit the ball foul, or miss it completely. So, my dad took things to another level.

We went to an open field with a bucket of baseballs. My dad pitched to me but told me not to swing. Instead, he wanted me to picture myself hitting the ball. Once I could imagine myself hitting the ball perfectly three times in a row, I could swing. It took about seven or eight pitches, but suddenly, something clicked. In my mind, I crushed the next pitch. Then another one and another one. When I finally swung my bat, I hit a towering home run. In fact, I hit five home runs on the next six swings. Suddenly, hitting a baseball felt like the easiest thing in the world.

That event had a significant impact on me. It taught me about the power of the brain. Later, I realized that the way we see ourselves is one of the most powerful forces in the world. When my self-talk and self-perception get off, it affects everything else I do.

This is one of the reasons why understanding our identity in Christ is so important. It has a major impact on the way we approach life. Just as I lost my ability to hit a baseball when the image in my head was broken but got my ability back when the picture got fixed, we can often see our whole life pivot by seeing ourselves as God sees us.

In the last chapter, we looked at what is legally and objectively true about us in Christ. That is an important part of shaping the way we see ourselves. In this chapter, I want to take this a step further and look at the other half of identity. Let's talk about the more subjective part of our identity that is based on attachment, comparison, and wounds from the past.

IDENTITY AND ATTACHMENT

From our brain's perspective, identity is always relational. This is an important concept to understand. It means there is an element to our identity in Christ that goes beyond what we know to be true and is connected to who we love. This is the other half of identity.

It is the right side of the brain that is primarily related to relational attachment. This means it is like an engine whose primary job is relationships. When this part of the brain is strong because we have lots of joyful relationships, we develop a strong and resilient sense of who we are.

From our brain's perspective, identity is always relational.

Without going into too much brain science, let me make two key observations about how the brain creates identity and attachment.

1. The Identity Center

The identity center of the brain is located at the pinnacle of its attachment system. The identity center is your brain's boss. When it is working properly, it helps us with a host of extremely important functions. Here are just a few of them:

- It remembers who I am, who my people are, and how we act under these conditions.
- It remembers the values that reflect who I am.
- It is creative, goal-oriented, and pursues satisfying activities.
- It provides my moral compass.
- It helps me calm upset emotions in both myself and others.[1]

The technical name of the identity center is the prefrontal cortex, and it is located behind the right eye. When this part of the brain gets damaged, people can forget who they are (amnesia) or stop acting like themselves because they forget how it is like them to act (this has been known to happen with gunshot wounds and other trauma to this region of the brain). It is significant that God chose to make our identity center the master and commander of the brain. This means God places a high value on being ourselves and growing our capacity to act like ourselves even when enduring hardship.

My identity center will always link my identity to my group. From my brain's perspective, I get my identity from my people. Knowing who my people are is the anchor of knowing who I am. This is true even at levels that may not be obvious. To say I am a man means I belong to a group of people called men. It comes with a set of expectations about how men are to act. To say I am a leader means I belong to a group known as leaders. It too comes with expectations about how we leaders do life.

For the Christian, the idea of group identity is huge. It means we need to train our brains to see our people as God's kingdom people above all other categories from which we could take our identity. Let me illustrate.

When Jesus taught the Sermon on the Mount, He had a lot to say about identity groups. In His day, there were many groups that loved their own people but didn't love those outside their group. The Pharisees and Sadducees didn't like each other. Jews and Samaritans were enemies. Tax collectors and the poor were natural adversaries. And, of course, there were the Romans. Jesus preached a radical message that we were to love and do good to those who were not our people. Those who followed Him were to become part of a new people who loved even their enemies. That is an amazing identity, and it is anchored in the fact that our people are kingdom people.

2. The Joy Center

The identity center of the brain is also the brain's joy center. That is good news because it means God designed us so that our true self is who we are when we are living with joy. Too many people define themselves by their shortcomings, malfunctions, and poor comparisons to others. But that is not who we really are. Our true identity is always related to joy.

I learned what I know about brain science from my friend Jim Wilder. He has a PhD in psychology and has devoted much of his professional career to researching the brain. According to Jim, our brains are designed by God to run on joy. This insight was originally discovered by Dr. Allan Schore, who has been called the Einstein of Psychoanalysis for his work on attachment and the brain.[2] I remember Jim saying how profound it was that a man as technical and clinical as Dr. Schore couldn't find a better word than joy to describe the fuel our brains crave.

It is often taught in Christian circles that joy is a choice. I think what people mean is that we can choose a different attitude or choose to think about different thoughts. However, from the brain's perspective, joy is not a choice. It is an emotion that is triggered when we know someone is happy to be with us. Think of it this way. A grandmother doesn't have to choose to light up or try to get a twinkle in her eye when her grandkids stop by her house. A boyfriend doesn't have to choose to feel a surge of joy when the girl he likes smiles at him. From a scientific perspective, joy is a high-energy reaction to a relational connection.

No one ever says, "You know what my problem is? I just have too much joy today." Nobody goes to therapy to try to decrease their joy. Our problems come when we lack joy.

Joy is meant to be the foundation of our sense of identity. As a child, if my people are generally happy to see me, I will feel secure in those relationships. I will see myself as someone people like, and I will usually learn to like myself. However, if my people are scary and unpredictable, I will likely struggle with my self-worth because my brain will learn to see myself as someone others have trouble liking. Attaching to people who are happy to see me creates joy bonds. Attaching to people who are not happy to see me creates fear bonds. All of this affects how well my identity center develops.

A problem that affects many Christians is growing up in families filled with fear bonds. When this happens, our brains get trained to bond in fear. This means that even relationships that don't have to be scary tend to be seen as scary. If we don't recognize what is happening and make some changes, we will turn all of our relationships into fear bonds. For example, if I have a brain that has learned to bond around fear, I will tend to focus on limiting damage in my relationships rather than maximizing joy. I constantly wait for the other shoe to drop, rather than anticipating we will be happy to see each other next time.

Some of us have a fear bond with our heavenly Father, and it will take some work to change that.

Fear bonds are especially problematic when it comes to God. Since joy is not a choice, I can't simply choose to be happy to be bonded to God. Some of us have a fear bond with our heavenly Father, and it will take some work to change that. One friend of mine who works with deeply traumatized people—many who have been abused by their fathers—teaches them to pray by talking to the Good Shepherd rather than the Father. She has found that relatively few Americans have been traumatized by shepherds. This slight adjustment can help them begin to form a joy bond with God while they are beginning to heal from their pain.

I learned about joy bonds and fear bonds in a workshop by Jim Wilder. After listening to his presentation, I realized I often struggled with fear bonds, including one with God. One of the characteristics of a fear bond is that we feel like we have to perform to be accepted. For example, if you know you are about to visit your parents and feel a surge of excitement, that is a joy bond. But if you know you are about to see your parents and you feel anxiety, that is a fear bond. Fear bonds often make you feel like you will have to be perfect or pretend to be someone you are not to be accepted.

I realized I had a fear bond with God one night when I started to pray. As I closed my eyes, I saw two theater masks: the one for comedy that is smiling and the one for tragedy that is crying. Only in my mind, the mask for tragedy was stern and angry. I realized that I didn't know if God was happy to see me or not. I remember saying, "Okay, God, which one is it? Are You happy to see me, or are You upset with me?" At the time, I had no tools for dealing with this, and I just stopped praying right there.

As time went by and I began to look for root causes of why I had a fear bond with God, I realized a few things. First, my early childhood experience of Christianity had both happy and scary elements to it.

For example, I liked going to church. I had friends there, and it was a happy place for me most of the time. I also enjoyed learning stories from the Bible. From an early age, I wanted to understand the big picture of how they all fit together. There was also a part of my heart that truly loved God.

On the other hand, most of the "mature" believers I knew were strict and rarely smiled. I got the impression that Christianity was serious business, not something anchored in joy. I also had some religious wounds from early childhood that made part of my heart not trust God at all. Thus, there were times when I was joy bonded to God, but times— when I got triggered—that fear drove my attachment to Him.

IDENTITY AND COMPARISON

Given the fact that identity is so foundational to our new life in Christ, it is not surprising that Satan tries to give us a counterfeit identity. He uses the world to provide us one based on the flesh.

The world is a system with a pecking order where the strong dominate the weak. To be strong in the world's eyes is to be beautiful, intelligent, influential, talented, and above those we consider weak. In the world's system, we gain our identity from our place in this pecking order. The beautiful and talented rarely have to do much more than show up to be accepted.

Most of us learn where we fit in the world's pecking order based on comparison. We look at ourselves, then look at someone else and think, "I'm not as good looking as she is," "I'm not as clever as he is," or "I'm not as influential as they are." But then, we look at someone else and tell ourselves, "I am at least better looking than him," or we feel more talented, have a higher status, or feel superior in some area of comparison. We then take our identity from how we see ourselves in relation to others. And, thanks to mediums like social media, we often don't even compare ourselves with real people. We create imaginary standards against which we compare ourselves.

There is an obvious problem with this system. It naturally leads to either pride or inferiority. Most of us struggle with a bit of both because, in some areas, we feel good about the way we compare, while in other areas, we don't. The other problem with this system is that it is anchored in the flesh. As God said to Samuel about David's brother Eliab, "Do not look on his appearance or on the height of his stature, because I have rejected him. For the LORD sees not as man sees: man looks on the outward appearance, but the LORD looks on the heart" (1 Sam. 16:7).

When I was in high school, I often struggled with my identity. One night I talked to my dad about it.

He took out a pad of paper, drew a line on it, and said, "The devil likes to drive us to extremes. He doesn't really care which extreme he drives us to as long as he can control us."

On one end of the line, he wrote "inferiority," and at the other end, he wrote "conceit." He then explained, "Conceit and inferiority are two extremes, but they come from the same source. They both come from looking at yourself and comparing yourself to others." He then wrote the word "self" underneath the line.

He continued, "Both of these extremes are counterfeits of God's intended virtues. Conceit is the counterfeit of confidence. Inferiority is the counterfeit of humility. Humility is not thinking badly of yourself or saying that you don't compare well to others. Humility is not thinking about yourself at all. It avoids the comparison game. In the same way, confidence is not about thinking you are better than others. It is about living life with the freedom that comes from seeing yourself the way God sees you." He paused and wrote the word "God" above the line.

GOD

Humility   **Confidence**

Inferiority   **Conceit**

SELF

He then explained:

When we fix our eyes on God and see ourselves the way He sees us, we live out of the twin virtues of humility and confidence rather than the twin counterfeits of inferiority and conceit.

On the one hand, when God looks at you, He remembers that

you are simply dust. There is no basis for conceit. Do you think you are good-looking? God can take that away in a moment. Are you smart? That is a gift that you did nothing to earn. When we remember that we are but dust, we lose any reason for conceit. Instead, we discover humility.

On the other hand, when God looks at you, He says, "This person is worth My Son's life." As Paul wrote, "He who did not spare His own Son, but gave Him up for us all—how will he not also, along with Him, graciously give us all things?" (Rom. 8:32 NIV). We live with the freedom of our confidence in how God sees us rather than the fleeting confidence of how we compare with others.[3]

The next day, when I went to school, I was determined to throw away the imaginary mirror I always seemed to carry with me. Instead of looking at my friends at school and wondering what they thought of me and how I compared to them, I saw them as dust of great worth. I saw myself that way and felt free to forget about myself and focus on them. It was like living in a new reality. I realized how much time I spent thinking about myself and what others thought of me. Without that baggage, I felt free, like I could see my friends for who they were for the first time. I didn't need to impress anyone. I just needed to love them, which was suddenly much easier than before.

> **Confidence is not about thinking you are better than others. It is about living life with the freedom that comes from seeing yourself the way God sees you.**

The world is a predatory place. The strong oppress the weak. They use their strength to keep themselves at the top of the pecking order. But the kingdom is not that way. In the kingdom of God, the strong serve the weak. Jesus said, "Anyone who wants to be first must be the very last, and the servant of all" (Mark 9:35 NIV).

IDENTITY AND WOUNDS FROM THE PAST

I have met with many people who have a fear bond with God. Such fear is always rooted in one of two types of trauma. It is either rooted in bad things that have happened to them (B Trauma—"B" as in bad), or it is rooted in good things they miss (A Trauma—"A" as in the absence of the good we need).[4]

A Trauma happens when we miss out on crucial developmental training. If no one stays relationally happy to be with us when we go through hard emotions, that is A Trauma. No one abused us, but no one was there for us in the way we needed them to be. In the same way, missing out on a skill like learning to speak French means that I will reach my adult years without that skill. So, every emotional and relational skill I miss getting as a child is still not there when I get older. The good news is that I can start where I am and still work with others to develop those skills.

Fear bonds with God are often formed by the WLVS pattern introduced in chapter 4. Various wounds from our past can lead to lies about God that cause us to make vows that keep us away from Him and produce strongholds in our lives. To explain what I mean, let's look at three common types of wounds: father wounds, mother wounds, and religious wounds.

Father Wounds

Father wounds are especially significant because they directly impact our identity. Nearly everyone who struggles with their sense of identity will find a father wound in their past. Sometimes this is a wound of A Trauma. Perhaps our father was simply emotionally unavailable to us. Maybe he was gone during our formative years or had abandoned the family. Sometimes this is a wound of B Trauma because our father was emotionally, physically, or even sexually abusive. When our view of our earthly father is significantly damaged by trauma, it is hard not to see our heavenly Father through a similar lens.

Mother Wounds

There can be A and B Trauma related to our mothers. When this happens, we often struggle to feel loved and feel especially alone in our upsetting emotions. If our mother was not emotionally or relationally available to us or her availability was conditional and had to be earned, that will profoundly impact our ability to feel lovable.

Religious Wounds

A religious wound is experienced in church or by a religious figure or by being introduced to concepts too deep for our age. For example, I know people who were abused in churches or by Christian leaders or people who did evil in the name of Jesus. Such wounds have an extra layer because they have a religious element that directly attacks our bond with God.

Many people have been wounded by spiritual abuse in the church. The list of ways that people have been damaged in the name of Jesus could fill the rest of this book. I know of one famous atheist who was sexually abused by his pastor. It is hard to blame such a person for having a jaded view of God. I think God understands this, and I trust Him to be merciful and just with such people.

Heart-focused discipleship is required to help people move from fear bonds to joy bonds with God.

Father, mother, and religious wounds require more than forgiveness to heal. There are skills we have missed that will have to be relearned. We may need a father figure or mother figure in our lives who can supply parts of what our birth parents did not or could not do for us. We will likely need emotional healing for the pockets of pain related to our B Trauma. For more help with this, I recommend starting with my book *Understanding the Wounded Heart* and the free video course that goes with it.[5]

The fear bonds caused by trauma are one of the most profound reasons why traditional discipleship is not enough. A discipleship process that does not address our fear bonds with God will always end up warped in one way or another. Heart-focused discipleship is required to help people move from fear bonds to joy bonds with God.

IDENTITY AND HEART VALUES

God made each of us unique. There is an identity anchored in what God has placed inside each one of us. To discover our unique heart identity, we usually need help. We need other people who know us well enough to see and affirm how God has made us. This goes beyond legal realities to individual realities.

We begin to recognize what makes us unique, both in what makes us come alive and what causes us great pain. For example, if I have a heart that values justice, I will be energized by stories of justice being served and truth prevailing. I will be motivated to work for causes that seek to bring justice to unjust situations. My passion for justice also means that it is especially painful to my heart when I see injustice prevailing. If I have a heart that values mercy, I will be energized by stories of those in need of mercy. I will be motivated to serve in ways that show mercy, and it will be especially painful to my heart to see people denied mercy. Most of us have a passion for what is good, but some of us are a bit more wired in one direction than another. Justice-motivated people tend to want to stand up for what is right. Mercy-motivated people want to reach out to those in need.

There are many more heart values than justice and mercy. Here is a short list to inspire your thinking:

- Creativity
- Beauty
- Organization
- Construction
- Teaching
- Healing
- Leading
- Protecting

At some level, all of our heart characteristics are related to love. They are the ways that God has wired us to want to make life better for others. Some of us like to fix things. Some like to make the world a more beautiful place. Some like to organize what is chaotic. Maybe you love hospitality or motivating others to make a difference in the world. Sometimes we recognize our passions and deep desires. But we also need others to see those qualities in us and serve as a mirror to see the heart God has given us.

For many years, I worked with a woman who had been bullied her whole life. She had suffered incredible rejection at school, church, and in her own family. She saw herself as having many characteristics—none of them good. She was labeled early on as a special needs kid and treated like she was stupid. The first person who really showed her attention and made her feel special ended up sexually abusing her.

For a long time, I never saw this woman's true heart. It was covered up by too much pain. But now and then, I could get a glimpse. She would get excited about a blind musician who played at Carnegie Hall or a special needs child whose family had helped them reach a dream. Her pain made her especially sensitive to those who were overlooked. When her true heart peeked out, it was filled with compassion.

In one appointment, she sensed the Lord calling her His "warrior princess." It became a theme in her healing journey. Jesus wanted to replace the identity the world had given her with the heart identity He had given her. The devil had seen the same heart values and tried to distort them. Her warrior nature came out in rage at others and a lifetime of being at war with the world. But Jesus began to remold that heart value into a warrior who fought first for her own freedom and then for the freedom of others. Her compassion came through whenever she saw someone who was oppressed and abused or neglected and mistreated. Her compassion

A healing journey requires others to see our hearts and find joy in what they see. It is what we all need.

could make her extremely gentle, and that is when the princess part would come to the surface. She loved filling people's worlds with beauty and seeing them smile.

A healing journey like hers requires others to see our hearts and find joy in what they see. It is what we all need.

PUTTING IT ALL TOGETHER

The question of our identity is, at its core, a worldview question. It is about who gets to define reality. Do we let our reality be defined by the world, the flesh, and the devil? Or, do we turn to God for the definitive answer to what is real? If I define myself by comparison to others or based on how I feel, I am using the world's system. When I look to God and say about myself what He says, I am dealing with reality as it actually is, from God's perspective. The good news here is that God thinks I am incredibly special.

Identity is the foundation on which we must build our lives. In Christ, we have a secure identity. But the world, wounds, and warfare often attack us at the level of how we see ourselves as Satan aims his cannons at the foundation of our lives. He knows that if he can take out the foundation, the rest of the structure will inevitably collapse.

As we turn our attention to Scripture, walking in the Spirit, and heart-focused community, we will find that they work together to keep our foundation strong. The Scriptures give us a worldview that helps us see God, ourselves, and life through a unique set of lenses. The Holy Spirit continually calls us to live out the identity He has given us. And a heart-focused community is often key to developing a strong identity foundation. It reminds us who we are and helps us live from the new heart that is ours in Christ.

CHAPTER 8

SPIRIT AND SCRIPTURE

MY FATHER HAD A DAILY FIVE-MINUTE radio spot for a few years called "Keeping Your Balance." In every episode, he stated his thesis that the Christian life is the exciting process of learning to keep your balance. The idea was that Satan is constantly trying to get us to go to extremes and lead us away from the balancing point of truth. For example, Satan doesn't really care if we move toward legalism or license, as long as he pushes us away from the true fulcrum of biblical grace. Or, when it comes to spiritual warfare, the devil doesn't really care if we think it is all nonsense or if we become occultists, as long as he keeps us from the true biblical center living from a place of victory.

When it comes to living in the Spirit, there is a balance that must be struck between the study of Scripture and the experience of hearing the Spirit's voice. You can think of Scripture and Spirit as the two wings of an airplane. Both are needed for the plane to keep its balance. Because the Holy Spirit is the one who inspired the authors of Scripture, the Bible cannot be separated from the idea of walking in the Spirit. It takes both a growing ability to recognize the Spirit's leading and the foundation and correction that comes from the Scriptures.

Some churches have been accused of preaching the Trinity as Father, Son, and Holy Bible. They are so focused on Scripture that they miss the Spirit and the spiritual realities to which the Scriptures point. Other churches have been accused of being so focused on the Holy Spirit that they treat the Scriptures flippantly. I have been to both kinds of churches.

One Holy Spirit-focused church invited a guest preacher to speak. His message was that if you gave money to the church building fund, you could guarantee your child's salvation. This person had helped a lot of churches raise a lot of money with his false promises. His text was God's statement to David that He would build David a house. In context, God is promising David a dynasty that will rule over Israel, culminating with the Messiah. It has nothing to do with the individual salvation of his descendants. God makes this promise in response to David's desire to build a house for God. So, the preacher combined these ideas and said that if we give money to build God a house, God will guarantee the salvation of our children. He also said that the Holy Spirit had given him this message to bring to the church.

This preacher's mishandling of Scripture was appalling. Yet no one at this church seemed to notice. They assumed that anyone with God's "anointing" must be teaching the truth. This is why it is so crucial to handle the Bible well and let it serve as a corrective to false teaching.

On the other extreme, we need to look no further than the Pharisees to find a prime example of people who were so trapped in their own theological system that no experience of the Spirit's power could convince them to take a second look at Scripture and see if they had mishandled it. No matter how many miracles Jesus performed or how much evidence there was for His resurrection, their rigid interpretation of Scripture blinded them to what was right in front of their eyes. In the same way, I have met Christians who have reduced their faith to reason and discipline. They have so watered down the role of the spirit world, they have no expectation for either the Holy Spirit or wicked spirits to have a direct impact on life.

As we look at the idea of walking in the Spirit, we will approach the subject with the idea of balance in mind. This chapter will deal with the Scripture, and the next chapter will deal with recognizing the Spirit's voice.

A LESSON FROM JOSHUA

After Moses died, Joshua took over as the leader of God's chosen people. He came to leadership at a crucial moment in the life of the nation. It would be his job to lead the invasion of the promised land to reclaim it from God's enemies. You might think that with a military mission, Joshua's focus would be on preparing his armies with the latest technology and training for battle. God gave him a different priority:

> "Be careful to obey all the law my servant Moses gave you; do not turn from it to the right or to the left, that you may be successful wherever you go. Keep this Book of the Law always on your lips; meditate on it day and night, so that you may be careful to do everything written in it. Then you will be prosperous and successful. Have I not commanded you? Be strong and courageous. Do not be afraid; do not be discouraged, for the LORD your God will be with you wherever you go." (Josh. 1:7–9 NIV)

The key to victory in the upcoming battles was not military excellence, but God's intervention. I sometimes say that Israel was an inept army, but they had a superweapon. When they obeyed, the Creator of the world, with all of His power and wisdom, promised to fight their battles. Victory had far less to do with their ability to fight than with the participation of the divine warrior they were called to trust.

Throughout the book of Joshua, we see that fear is what God intended for His enemies. It belonged in their camp. Fearlessness and courage were to be the characteristics of God's people. If He told them to fight, there was no battle they could not win. Joshua's top priority needed to be obedience to God's will so that God would fight with Israel and against her enemies. When God fights, God wins. The model is clear.

MEMORIZATION AND MEDITATION HELP US OBEY

God needed Joshua to trust Him enough to obey Him. My dad used to put it this way: "Do things God's way, and God will be responsible for the results. Do things your way, and you can be responsible for the results."

To make sure Joshua did things God's way, God told him to meditate on the book of the law day and night. The Hebrew word for *meditate* means "to mutter." It creates the image of a person muttering what they have memorized under their breath. If Joshua obeyed this command, he would have memorized the entire law in a few years.

If obedience is the key to victory, then meditation on Scripture is the chain that holds this key around our necks, so we remember to use it.

God had Joshua meditate on the law day and night, so He would grow his trust and remember to obey.

As we make Bible memorization and meditation a regular part of our daily routine, something happens inside of us.

Having God's Word hidden in our hearts is crucial to our walk with Him. One of the most foundational practices I ever developed was Bible memorization. From age eighteen to twenty-four, I memorized about two-thirds of the New Testament through a program called Bible Quizzing. It was not uncommon for me to spend ten to twenty hours each week memorizing and meditating on Scripture. (See Appendix 2 for a few tips I picked up for memorizing entire passages of Scripture.)

As we make Bible memorization and meditation a regular part of our daily routine, something happens inside of us. Our story becomes an extension of Scripture's story. We begin seeing the events in our lives through its lens. The worldview of the Bible becomes our worldview that guides our values and behaviors.

The practice of biblical meditation also keeps God in our thoughts and makes trust easier. The many stories of how God came through against all odds and won the day for His people begin to mold our approach to life. We start to expect that life will be hard and full of battles, but that God will face each battle with us and that, in the end, ours will be a story of redemption.

TRUST PLUS OBEDIENCE EQUALS VICTORY

Trust is a relational word. If I trust you, it means that even if I don't understand everything you are up to, I will give you the benefit of the doubt. If I trust God, it means that even if I don't understand why He is allowing pain into my life, I trust He has a plan and that He is present with me through it.

Most Christians who struggle to trust God have a fear bond with Him rather than a joy bond. I have a friend who lived through tremendous childhood abuse at the hands of her father. It was the kind of trauma that leads to the creation of multiple personalities (or dissociative identity disorder).

As an older child, she became a Christian and went to church. A Sunday School teacher told her that if she had faith, she could ask God for anything, and He would do it. With childlike faith, she asked God to stop the abuse. It didn't work. Her dad didn't stop selling her to his buddies as a sex toy. Talk about a crisis of faith. How do you trust God when you ask Him to stop your abuse, and He doesn't do it?

Today, my friend runs a ministry for those who have endured sex trafficking as she did. The journey that got her to the point where she was able to help others build their trust in God had many stops along the way. It was not quick, and it was not easy.

However, one of the gifts God gave her as a young teen was something she calls "the unexplained box." It was a mental box where she could put all the stuff she couldn't explain, like why God would let her endure such trauma. The idea was that someday, God would give her more insight into these questions. In the meantime, He wanted her to know that she could trust Him. He had a plan. He was present and had not abandoned her. It proved to be true. While her life is still hard, she lives with as much joy and peace as anyone I know.

JOSHUA AND LIVING IN THE SPIRIT

Not only does Joshua point us to meditation on God's Word for the wisdom we need, but the book also models listening prayer and the importance of a relational walk with God. Joshua fought many battles. God did not simply give him a textbook and say, "Here are all the principles you need in order to win all these battles." God's approach was much more relational. He wanted Joshua to seek Him, listen for His guidance, and then obey what he heard and watch what happened. When Joshua did this, he always won the battle. In the next chapter, I will unpack this some more, but for now, let me point out the steps in what Joshua did:

- **Seek**—He took time to ask for God's strategy for each new problem or battle that came his way. When he didn't take time to seek God, it led to more problems.
- **Listen**—He waited until he heard from God and had God's guidance before he acted.
- **Obey**—Once Joshua knew what God wanted him to do, he obeyed. Obedience became the key to victory in the battles he fought.
- **Watch**—Joshua got to watch what happened when he did things God's way. He also got to see what happened when he forgot to seek God and listen for His guidance. The classic example of this was when the Gibeonites pretended to be foreigners who had traveled a great distance, and Joshua did not seek the Lord before

entering into a pact with them (Josh. 9–10). It led to all sorts of problems.

The next chapter will focus more on SLOW and how to develop a listening prayer life that seeks God's guidance. For now, I want to take you on a quick overview of the nine building blocks of biblical theology that help us understand the big picture of what is going on in the Bible.

THE BIG PICTURE

The Bible is a big book. It would intimidate almost anyone. It can help to get a handle on the big picture of how it all fits together. In the remainder of this chapter, I don't want to go through the basics of how many books are in the Bible and how it is organized. You can get that almost anywhere. I want to focus on nine building blocks that summarize the theology of the Bible.

The purpose of life is worship. We were created to walk with God.

Not shockingly (as you see the way I teach), you can remember these building blocks with an acronym. In this case, I use a web address: www.plaxn.com. As of the writing of this book, that website actually works. Here is the idea it is meant to communicate.

Creation Theology

Creation theology refers to lessons directly related to the worldview on which the Bible is based. The first three building blocks can be remembered with the letters WWW. They represent three foundational elements of a biblical worldview: worship, warfare, and wisdom. One of the reasons these elements are paired together is that they are all anchored in lessons from creation. Thus, scholars sometimes refer to these elements as creation theology.

Worship. The purpose of life is worship. We were created to walk with God. When the Bible describes a relationship with God, it doesn't use the word *relationship*. Instead, it uses the image of walking. Adam and Eve walked with God in the garden of Eden (Gen. 3:8). Enoch walked with God and is a model of the sort of life God desires (Gen. 5:22). Noah walked with God and was found righteous in His sight (Gen. 6:9).

The type of worship God seeks is that of walking humbly with Him and treating our neighbors with justice and mercy (Mic. 6:8). To say we were created for worship is another way of saying we were made for walking with God in trust and obedience.

Years ago, a holocaust survivor named Corrie ten Boom modeled what it looks like to walk closely with God even through great tragedy. She is attributed with saying these words about the value of an intimate walk with God: "If you look at the world, you'll be distressed. If you look within, you'll be depressed. If you look at God, you'll be at rest."[1]

Warfare. The Bible is clear that we live in "the present evil age" (Gal. 1:4). This evil age began because of Adam and Eve's rebellion and will continue until the rebellion ends and the kingdom of God is established on earth. This evil age is a time of war. We are all born into a world at war. Indeed, you cannot understand life apart from this reality.

Jesus taught us to pray, "Your kingdom come, your will be done, on earth as it is in heaven" (Matt. 6:10). One of the reasons He taught us to ask for God's will to be done on earth is that it is often not done. Injustice is never God's desire, and yet it happens routinely. We pray that God's kingdom will come because—when that

---

Nine Building Blocks of

BIBLICAL THEOLOGY

Worship

Warfare

Wisdom

Promise

Law

Anointed One

X – Exile

New Covenant

Coming of Messiah

happens—all injustice will cease. God's purposes for creation will be completely fulfilled. In the meantime, we live in a world at war.

One of Satan's favorite strategies is to cause evil and suffering, then convince us that God is to blame. However, the Bible is clear on three points:

1. God allows evil.
2. God uses evil.
3. God overcomes evil.

We see these illustrated clearly in the life of the patriarch Joseph:

- **God allows evil.** God allowed Joseph to be treated with great injustice. He was unjustly sold into slavery by his brothers. As a slave, he was unjustly thrown into prison because a powerful person lied about him. As a prisoner, he was unjustly abandoned because people he helped forgot about him. Joseph had every reason to be angry with God. But he apparently had "an unexplained box," just like the teen I told you about earlier did. He was able to put the evil that had happened to him in that box and continue to trust God.
- **God uses evil.** God used the evil Joseph endured to put him into position to accomplish enormous good. Joseph was able to establish a system of food distribution that saved Egypt and kept his family alive during a seven-year famine. Joseph told his brothers, "You intended to harm me, but God intended it for good to accomplish what is now being done, the saving of many lives. So then, don't be afraid. I will provide for you and your children" (Gen. 50:20–21 NIV).
- **God overcomes evil.** In the end, God overcame the evil that was done to Joseph. He gave him a position of authority second only to Pharaoh in the land of Egypt. God also blessed Joseph with a family of his own and reconciliation with the family of his birth.

In the end, Joseph became a great person whose final years were filled with blessings.

Unless we understand that we live in a world at war, we will not be able to see God's hand in allowing, using, and overcoming evil in our lives.

A biblical worldview informs us that there is an unseen realm filled with supernatural beings. Paul wrote, "For we do not wrestle against flesh and blood, but against principalities, against powers . . ." (Eph. 6:12 NKJV). He doesn't simply say that we wrestle with demons or Satan. The idea of principalities is that there are supernatural forces which can be thought of as rulers over people and regions (such as the prince of Persia and the prince of Greece, as mentioned in Daniel 10:20). The term *powers* relates to the fact that many of these spirits have power over aspects of nature. Paganism was anchored in the worship of these principalities and powers. From this perspective, evangelism is about invading enemy territory, and discipleship involves reclaiming surrendered ground from the enemy. This is why freedom, as we've talked about, plays such a key role in the discipleship process.

Wisdom. The third foundational element of a biblical worldview is wisdom. In this fallen world, we need a guide. God has given us two gifts that work together to teach us wisdom. He has given us Scripture and the Spirit. Without the Spirit, Scripture can be easily manipulated and used to harm people. Without the Scripture, people can easily be led astray by emotional or supernatural experiences. I sometimes think of the Scripture and the Spirit as God's lantern for guiding us through this dark world. The Scripture is the frame of the lantern, and the Spirit is the flame. Together they serve as a light to our path.

In the Bible, there is a cluster of words related to wisdom:

- Blessing and cursing
- Good and evil
- Life and death

The book of Psalms begins with the word "blessed" (Ps. 1:1). It teaches us that if we want a blessed life (one that ends in what is good and in life rather than one that ends under God's curse so that we experience evil and death), we need to meditate on God's law and put it into practice. The Sermon on the Mount follows a similar pattern. It opens with eight statements of the kind of life God blesses (we call these the Beatitudes). The sermon ends with a parable about wisdom and how fools hear Christ's words but do not put them into practice, while the wise listen and obey, thus building their house on a rock that can withstand the storms of life (Matt. 7:24–27).

Throughout the Bible, wisdom has two main elements: discernment and discipline. Discernment is the ability to distinguish between what is good for me and what will end in evil. It recognizes which path God will bless and which path He will curse. Discipline refers to doing what wisdom has taught us will end in blessing, goodness, and life.

From a biblical perspective, a fool is one who does not trust God's wisdom but relies on his own understanding instead. The classic example of this in Scripture is the prodigal son (Luke 15:11–32). This young man was a textbook fool. His discernment was off, and so was his discipline. He thought he knew where to find "the good life." All he needed was his freedom and some money. However, the path he thought would lead to life (good) ended in disaster (evil). In the end, he repented of his folly and became wise by returning to the source of true blessing.

God gave us the Scriptures and the Spirit so that we would have a source of wisdom to guide us through this fallen world. Wisdom is embodied in the same formula we saw in Joshua. Trust plus obedience equals blessing. God says that the good life—a life blessed by Him—is found on the path of trusting what He says and obeying it.

Salvation Theology

Now that we have explored creation theology, we need to take a look at salvation theology. This refers to God's plan to bring salvation to the world that was gradually unveiled in a series of covenants. You can remember these covenants with the word PLAN. (Look at the following image and chart.) You may notice that I have added an X to the word plan to spell PLAXN. The X represents the exile. While this is not a covenant, it is an event that is directly related to the covenants, so we need to understand its theological significance.

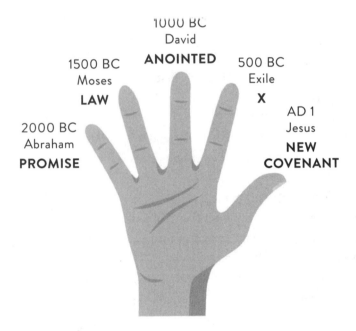

To begin, hold up your right hand and turn your palm toward your face. We will use each finger to remember one of the covenants.

Finger	Approx. Date	Name	Covenant
Pinkie	2000 BC[2]	Abraham	Promise
Ring Finger	1500 BC[3]	Moses	Law
Middle Finger	1000 BC[4]	David	Anointed One
Pointer	500 BC[5]	Exile	X
Thumb	AD 1[6]	Jesus	New Covenant

Promise. The first covenant is called the Promise (Gal. 3:17–18). It is also called the Abrahamic Covenant because it was made with Abraham. In Galatians 3:8, Paul referred to the Promise as the gospel preached ahead of time in the Old Testament. What did he mean? The Promise preached the gospel by declaring that through Abraham's family, God would send a seed (Jesus) and that all nations on earth would be blessed through Him (salvation would be made available to all nations [Gen. 22:18]).

In case there was any doubt about the meaning of these words, notice what was happening in Genesis 22 when God said them. The scene foreshadows the work of Christ on the cross. Abraham took his heir—the son he loved—and prepared to offer him as a sacrifice. At the last minute, God stopped him and provided a ram as

Just as the gospel must be received by faith, the Promise was not something to obey but something to be believed.

a substitute. The imagery foreshadows how God offered His beloved son as a sacrifice as a substitute for all who believe. The Promise to Abraham was the gospel preached ahead of time because it foretold that a seed (son) would come through Abraham's family and bring salvation to the nations.

Today, as foretold in this covenant, there are followers of Jesus in every nation of the world. The gospel is the fulfillment of the Promise.

Just as the gospel must be received by faith, the Promise was not something to obey but something to be believed.

Law. The second covenant is called the law or the Mosaic covenant. It was a covenant between God and Israel that was mediated by Moses. After Moses led the people out of Egypt, he took them to Mount Sinai. At this mountain something like a wedding ceremony took place. Moses was the officiating minister. Yahweh descended from heaven to the top of the mountain in an awesome display of power. The people gathered in the valley below in fear of the awesome sight they were seeing. Moses had built an altar at the base of the mountain. He took the blood of a bull and poured it into two bowls. God gave the people the Ten Commandments. If they promised to obey these commandments, He would make them His treasured possession so that out of all the nations on earth, they would belong uniquely to Him. The people agreed to obey and to serve no other gods but Yahweh.

I often picture Moses looking to the people and asking, "Do you, Israel, take Yahweh to be your God, forsaking all others to be His faithful wife?" The people said, "We do," and Moses confirmed their entry into the covenant by sprinkling the blood of a bull over the crowd. Then He asked God, "Do you, Yahweh, take Israel to be your wife and your treasured possession?" He said yes, and Moses poured the blood of a bull on the altar to represent God's entry into this amazing covenant relationship.

In a sense, the law was a wedding covenant. Israel agreed to obey her new husband and abandon the worship of all other gods. However, the history of Israel was a history of unbroken adultery. While still on their honeymoon at Mount Sinai, Israel built a golden calf and worshiped it. Throughout its history, there was immense pressure to be like the rest of the nations and worship many gods. Progressive thinkers despised the idea of exclusively worshiping one God. They thought it was wise to appease all the gods and folly to trust in only one. Thus, they turned the wisdom of the law upside down.

Anointed One. God made the third covenant with David. It guaranteed David a family dynasty and a "seed" who would rule forever. This seed was called the Anointed One. The Hebrew word for Anointed One is *meshiach*, from which we get the word "Messiah." The Greek word for Anointed One is *christos*, which gives us the word "Christ." Thus, David was promised that the Messiah (Christ) would come through his family line and reign forever.

Exile. Eventually, after generations of adultery and injustice, God sent the people into exile. The "x" in "plaxn" stands for exile. Both Isaiah and Jeremiah referred to the exile as a divorce (Isa. 50:1; Jer. 3:8). God sent His faithless wife away and issued her a certificate of divorce. However, God still loved His wife. He didn't want the relationship to end.

Out of sheer grace, He promised to establish a new covenant (Jer. 31; Ezek. 37). The new covenant would not be like the old covenant of the law, but instead like the original covenant of the Promise in that it would provide a relationship to be received by faith. However, this covenant would be even better than the Promise because instead of making only one nation God's elect people, it opened the door to all nations to join God's people.

New Covenant. The fourth covenant is simply called the new covenant. It fulfills the first three covenants and, in a sense, replaces them all by bringing them together in one. The new covenant was established by Jesus the Messiah. He is the seed promised to Abraham through whom all nations would be blessed. He is the seed promised to David who will reign forever. The new covenant replaces the old covenant (the law) and is superior to that covenant in every way. The epistle to the Hebrews is devoted to this theme.

As we saw in chapter 6 on our identity in Christ, the new covenant defines what is legally true of us in Christ. The Spirit's job is to bring what is legally true to life in us as we learn to walk in the Spirit. Thus, the new covenant, grace, and Spirit are all intimately connected.

COMING OF THE MESSIAH

.COM reminds us of the coming of the Messiah when His kingdom will be established on earth. The great hope of the Christian is that this world is not all there is. As Paul wrote, "If only for this life we have hope in Christ, we are of all people most to be pitied" (1 Cor. 15:19 NIV).

As we talked about in an earlier chapter, God's purpose was always to create a family in heaven and a family on earth and for the two of them to live together in unity under the reign of Christ. God's plan to fulfill that purpose has gone through many stages. The new covenant introduced what has been described as the "already" part of the kingdom of God. This means that some things have already changed because of what Jesus did when He came to earth the first time. These things have already been made new. There is another part of God's plan that has "not yet" happened. This "not yet" part of the plan is awaiting Christ's return and the creation of new heavens and a new earth (2 Peter 3:13).

There is a common misconception that Christians spend eternity in heaven and people get stuck thinking about clouds, harps, and choirs. But that is not how the Bible describes the coming kingdom. What people usually think of as heaven is the unseen realm where God has His throne today. It is described in Revelation 4–5. However, we do not spend eternity there. On the contrary, in Revelation 21, we read that God brings the throne room to earth to spend eternity here with us. In the end, His family in heaven and His family on earth will spend eternity together— angels and humans alike—all under the reign of Christ (Eph.1:10).

PEOPLE OF THE BOOK

I know this chapter has covered a lot of ground. It is basically a summary of biblical theology, which is hard to do quickly. However, I hope it has helped you get a firmer grasp of the big picture of what is going on in the Bible and perhaps inspired you to dive more deeply into it for yourself.

The Holy Spirit is the ultimate author of the Bible, having inspired those who wrote it (2 Tim. 3:16; 2 Peter 1:21) so that its words are trustworthy and true (John 17:17). The Bible forms the foundation of what we believe and provides a framework to keep us from straying into

error. Not that we are infallible in our
interpretation of Scripture, but having
an objective text to refer to creates an
authoritative reference point for our
understanding.

Every disciple must be a student of the Bible. We don't all have to be scholars, but we all have to be students.

The Scriptures and the Holy Spirit work together to guide us into the wisdom we need to navigate this fallen world. Every disciple must be a student of the Bible. We don't all have to be scholars, but we all have to be students.

Recently a missionary told of smuggling some Bibles into a region where the New Testament is forbidden. After dropping them off with a local member of the underground church, he asked if they wanted his team to come and do some teaching. The local Christian simply replied, "Book will teach," and left. The missionary had to smile. It was hard to argue with that.

CHAPTER 9

LIVING IN
THE SPIRIT

MOST OF US KNOW the story of Adam and Eve and how there were two trees in the garden of Eden. We usually know this as a temptation story, but there is more to it. The story of the garden of Eden is also about wisdom. The two trees tell a story with their names.

The first tree—the tree of life—reveals the goal or purpose of wisdom. We want to find life—a life that is good, blessed, abundant, and eternal. This has been the core question of humans in every age, "What is the good life and how do I get it?"

The second tree—the tree of the knowledge of good and evil—describes the nature of wisdom. Wisdom requires the ability to distinguish between good and evil. This isn't just about morals, though it is related. This is about recognizing what is good for me because it ends in the good life I'm looking for and what is bad for me because, well, it ends badly.

So, why start a chapter on walking in the Spirit with a discussion of wisdom and the garden of Eden? It is because what the Old Testament calls wisdom, the New Testament calls walking in the Spirit.

Wisdom always involves a choice. In Proverbs, two women call for us to follow them. One is wisdom, the other is folly. We have to choose. "There is a way that appears to be right, but in the end it leads to death" (Prov. 14:12 NIV). In the New Testament, Jesus said that there was a wide path and a narrow path (Matt. 7:13). One is the path of folly, and it leads to destruction. The other is the path of wisdom, and it leads to life.

In both the Old and New Testaments, the heart of wisdom is faith. Proverbs 3:5–6 reads, "Trust in the LORD with all your heart, and lean not on your own understanding; in all your ways acknowledge [or be intimate with][1] Him, and He shall direct your paths" (NKJV). In the New Testament, life in the Spirit is described as a walk of faith. Paul put it succinctly in 2 Corinthians 5:7, "For we live by faith, not by sight" (NIV). Trust is a very relational word. It is more than a choice to obey God. It is a bond with God that says, "I trust you more than I trust what I can see and understand for myself."

Wisdom is ultimately measured by eternity. When we order our lives in a way that pleases God, the wisdom of trusting God will be proven for all to see.

In both the Old and New Testaments, the Spirit is the source of all wisdom, whether it comes through revelation (dreams, visions, angels, prophecies, etc.) or whether it comes through Spirit-inspired Scripture. All wisdom flows from the Spirit of wisdom (Deut. 34:9; Eph. 1:17). Throughout the entire Bible, to be filled with God's Spirit is connected to being given wisdom from above (Ex. 31:3; 35:31; Deut. 34:9; Isa. 11:2; Dan. 5:11, 14; Acts 6:3, 10; 1 Cor. 2:13; 12:8; Eph. 1:17; Col. 1:9; 3:16).

Wisdom is ultimately measured by eternity. The one who orders his life in a way that pleases God may still suffer in this world, but in the end, the wisdom of trusting God will be proven for all to see. When those who relied on their own understanding are left ruined and destitute, and those who trusted God and obeyed Him are welcomed into paradise, there will be little question left about which was the wise way to live.

In the last chapter, we focused on the importance of the Bible and meditating on God's Word for growing our trust in Him. This chapter will look at the importance of developing a relationship of trust with God that is characterized by hearing His voice and obeying Him.

SLOW

Throughout history, godly men and women have stressed the importance of developing the kind of intimacy with God that allows us to recognize His voice. I did not grow up in a church that talked about hearing God's voice for ourselves. We were taught that the Bible was all we needed. This teaching is often true of left-brain, traditional discipleship. Its approach to Christianity is comfortable with study and reason and making good choices but generally misses the relational elements of the faith.

As a young pastor, I asked an older pastor who had a reputation for hearing from God what that meant and how I could learn to hear God's voice. He pointed me to 1 Corinthians 10:13, which says, "No temptation has overtaken you except what is common to mankind. And God is faithful; he will not let you be tempted [or tested] beyond what you can bear [to endure]. But when you are tempted, he will also provide a way out so that you can endure it" (NIV). Then he told me, "The next time you are tempted, do this: stop and listen. There will be a still, small voice inside showing you the way of escape. Listen to that voice." That was simple and straightforward.

Not long after that conversation, I had a chance to practice this pastor's advice. I got into an argument with a friend at church. He was upset with me and blamed me for something I did not think was my fault. I was getting angry. I could feel my face getting hot and my neck getting stiff. I was about to defend myself with anger when I remembered the pastor's words, "The next time you are tempted, stop and listen."

So, in my mind, I said a very spiritual prayer, "Okay, fine." God knew what I meant. I was willing to stop and listen.

Suddenly a surprising thought entered my mind. It was a Bible reference. The thought in my head was, "James 1:20." When I say the thought was surprising, I'm not kidding. It caught me off guard and distracted me from my argument. I didn't know what James 1:20 said. So, I stopped paying attention to my friend and started sorting through the file cabinet in my brain to see if I could remember the verse. Then I remembered. In fifth grade, we had memorized that verse at the private Christian school I attended. It says, "For the anger [or wrath] of man does not produce the righteousness of God."

I quickly went from the delight that I had remembered the verse to shame as I realized it applied to me. God was telling me that my anger would not accomplish His righteous purposes in this situation. However, my temper was already ignited, and I was fully in the flesh at that point, so I said another prayer in my mind. I prayed, "God, could you be more specific?"

God is patient. Another reference came to my mind. This one was Proverbs 15:1. I knew that one from eighth-grade Bible memory work. It says, "A gentle answer turns away wrath" (NIV). My internal reaction was something like, "Darn it. There is no getting out of this."

God had given me a more specific answer. He did not want me to use anger to handle this argument. Instead, He wanted me to give a gentle answer. I took a deep breath and did my best to obey. I said something like, "So, it seems like you are facing a really big problem, and you think it is all my fault."

At this, my friend took a step back as if he had been punched in the gut. He paused and said, "I guess you are right. I'm just really angry, and I'm taking it all out on you. I'm sorry."

A Simple Model for
WALKING IN THE SPIRIT
Seek (Stop)
Listen
Obey
Watch

A gentle answer had turned away his wrath. I must admit that I was actually a little disappointed. I was really looking forward to defending myself. But as I calmed down, I realized that God had just taken me through a practical exercise in hearing His voice.

We seek God by asking Him questions.

The pattern I learned from 1 Corinthians 10:13 led me back to Joshua. Just as Joshua had to learn to seek the Lord, listen to Him, obey Him, and watch what He did, so that is what I need to learn to do in order to walk in the Spirit. Here is the pattern we saw in the last chapter:

- Seek (Stop)
- Listen
- Obey
- Watch

We saw that Joshua meditated on the Torah as part of what helped him walk with God and be wise. We also saw that Joshua did more than meditate on the Bible. He also stopped what he was doing, sought the Lord, and listened for His guidance. In Hebrew, the words translated *seek* (*darash* and *baqash*) both carry the idea of "inquiring" or asking God questions. We seek God by asking Him questions.

Stopping and seeking are related. We need to stop what we are doing to seek God. We don't just do this when we are tempted. We do this as a regular part of our routine and as a regular part of dealing with the unexpected.

Have you ever thought about the idea that God designed time? He is not bound by it. He created the whole system by which we experience the passing of time. He made a planet that orbits the sun and spins on its axis. He created a moon to orbit the earth. He designed all of this and established it as a means of ordering our world.

In the Torah, God anchored the ceremonial calendar around the

156 A DEEPER WALK

times and seasons measured by the stars and the system of movement in the sky He ordained. Every month started with the new moon—the day on which the first sliver of light reappeared on the edge of the moon after it went dark. On that day, a double sacrifice was to be offered in worship. Every season—at times measured by astral experiences like an equinox or a solstice—there would be regular weeks devoted to worship. In addition, God ordained a weekly Sabbath. In fact, if you rested on every day that the Torah tells us not to work, seventy days of the year would be devoted to rest. That is fully 20 percent of the Jewish calendar year. In those days, people stopped their normal routines and sought the Lord in a more focused way.

> Every time we see a sunrise or a sunset, it is a call to worship.

We live in a world full of stress. Can you imagine how helpful it would be to devote seventy days a year to seek God as we stop all the normal activity that consumes our lives? God laid out a game plan to establish a rhythm of rest to help us have the capacity to handle the hardships of life. In addition, I find it interesting that God ordained a morning and an evening sacrifice. He also made the sunrise and sunset a spectacular experience. Every time we see a sunrise or a sunset, it is a call to worship. It is a reminder that God wants us to stop other things and seek Him. He wants us to have a relationship. He wants us to get to know Him well enough to trust Him so that we can live wisely and receive His blessing.

LEFT-BRAIN HEARING

In my experience, there are two main ways we hear God. One can be thought of as left-brain hearing, and the other as right-brain hearing. We tend to experience left-brain hearing as clear, distinct thoughts or images. Dreams would fit into this category. So would visions. What I experienced when I stopped to listen in a time of temptation was a clear, distinct thought. Let me give you a few examples.

When I served as a pastor, I often met with people for marriage counseling. One of the exercises I had them do was to stop and ask God two questions:

1. In words or pictures, how does the devil want me to see my spouse?
2. In words or pictures, how does the Holy Spirit want me to see my spouse?

One of the first times I tried this was with a woman who blamed her husband for all of her problems. She stopped, closed her eyes, and asked God the first question.

After about fifteen seconds, I asked, "What was the first thought you had or image you saw?"

She said, "I saw a ball and chain."

"What does that mean to you?" I asked.

She said, "I feel like I am ready to fly, and my husband is a ball and chain holding me back."

The irony was clear. This couple was from a generation that had often heard men refer to their wives as "the old ball and chain." I reminded her that this was an answer to the question, "How does the devil want me to see my husband?" and suggested she ask the second question.

She closed her eyes and asked how the Spirit wanted her to see her husband. Again, I asked what had come to her mind, and she said, "I saw a little boy standing with his head down facing an angry father."

> **God's thoughts are usually clear and distinct. They are usually surprising. And they always lead me to the fruit of the Spirit.**

"What does that mean to you?" I asked.

She said, "It means God wants me to see my husband as someone damaged by trauma who needs help and not to see him as my enemy."

Can you see how one narrative leads to division and one leads to love? When you push into this, it is often not hard to tell whether a thought is coming from God or the devil. God's thoughts lead us to the fruit of the Spirit. They bring us peace. They make us more loving, help us find joy, and so on.

Through my own experience and the experiences of others, I have learned that God's thoughts are usually clear and distinct. They are usually surprising. And they always lead me to the fruit of the Spirit.

Early in my marriage, I found myself waiting tables to pay the bills. It was a bit humbling because I had already earned two master's degrees and was working on a doctorate at that point. Plus, I had spent four years teaching at the college level.

One of my coworkers knew some of this and asked me bluntly, "What are you doing here, man?"

I said something about needing to take care of my family during this season of life, but in my mind, I heard the surprising, clear thought, "You are the only pastor these people are ever going to know." I didn't repeat that to my coworker, but it made an impression.

Later, I discussed it with my wife and friends. We all agreed that God was affirming that He had, in fact, called me to be a pastor and that He was giving me a ministry to the people at this restaurant.

In the two years I worked there, I spent time helping most of the people there process some of the hard things going on in their lives. We had some of them over for dinner. We included one of them in our Thanksgiving plans the year he went through a divorce. My wife and I were able to offer pastoral care to these hurting people.

RIGHT-BRAIN HEARING

Whereas left-brain hearing is about surprising, clear, and distinct thoughts or images, right-brain hearing is what my friend Jim Wilder calls "a mutual mind experience with God" or "thinking with God."[2] In our everyday lives, we communicate without words all the time. Most of it involves reading other people's body language and sending signals with our own. We think of it as sending and receiving signals. Sometimes we do it on purpose. Sometimes, we don't realize it is happening.

A mutual mind experience means that we are sharing the same thought. If I look at you and we make eye contact, I can communicate all sorts of messages to you nonverbally. I may roll my eyes like I am disgusted with something that was said. I may wink and nod like we understand each other. I may simply smile at you with a twinkle in my eye to let you know I like you. There are all sorts of messages that can be shared nonverbally.

When we sense what the other person is trying to communicate, we call that a mutual-mind experience. Sometimes when we get excited in a conversation where we are both brainstorming about ideas, it can be hard later to remember who had the idea first, because in many ways it was the collaboration that created the idea and we were creating and sharing it together.

God often speaks to us without words. We might call this having a sense that God wants us to do something or having peace about a decision. Sometimes, after we think about it for a while, we can put what we are sensing into words. We didn't receive the communication with words, but we understood the communication and can explain it to someone else if necessary. And, when we are meditating on and memorizing Scripture, it isn't hard for us to discern that what we're sensing is from God.

When my wife and I were seeking God's wisdom about whether to go out on our own and launch a new ministry, we set aside a couple of days for prayer and fasting to seek God and ask, "Do You want us to start this ministry?"

We were planning to call it Deeper Walk Ministries. The idea had come as I reflected on my years as a pastor and asked God to bring to mind the names of people who had experienced a deeper walk because of my ministry.

As I asked God this question, several names came to mind of people who had experienced significant life change in the prior seven years.

Then I asked, "What made the difference? Why did they experience so much transformation?"

As I listened, three thoughts came to mind:

1. They improved their biblical literacy.
2. They dealt with their emotional baggage.
3. They learned to walk in the Spirit.

These three elements became the core of the new ministry idea. We wanted to help people live with greater biblical literacy, greater emotional healing, and a greater experience of life in the Spirit. However, there is a big difference between having a ministry idea and being called to actually launch it.

That first night, my wife woke up in the middle of the night and journaled for an hour. She left with a clear sense that this was a calling. When she left for work the next morning, the last thing she said to me was, "We can do this." That stuck with me, because it was not like her to say that. She would normally say, "If this is what God wants, it will all work out," or something a little less direct.

That night I was playing Solitaire on the computer when I felt a Holy Spirit nudge. It didn't come as words or images, just a sense that I needed to stop wasting time and go seek God.

I left the room and opened my Bible. It fell open to Numbers 13–14. It was the story of the twelve spies as the people of Israel were trying to decide whether to invade the land or not. So, I started to read. When I came to Numbers 13:30 the words jumped off the page: "Then Caleb silenced the people before Moses and said, 'We should go up and take possession of the land, for we can certainly do it'" (NIV).

I shook my head and smiled broadly as I remembered my wife's words, "We can do this." Caleb had told the Israelites the same thing, "We can certainly do it!" I felt like I had my answer.

We began to put together a board and raise funds to launch a new ministry. Six months later, an established national ministry invited me to serve as their new president. When they heard about the discipleship model I had developed, their board said, "We want to do that here. You don't have to change a thing."

Sometimes God speaks with a right-brain, mutual-mind connection, in which we're able to think God's thoughts with Him.

In less than a year, God had turned my life around in ways I could never have seen coming. The next year, the ministry changed its name to Deeper Walk International, and I now have served as the president for over fifteen years.

God didn't speak to me in a left-brain, clear, distinct thought about starting a new ministry. It was a right-brain, mutual-mind connection, in which I was able to think God's thoughts with Him. Jim Wilder and colleagues call this "thought rhyming."[3] It is based on the idea that Hebrew poetry doesn't rhyme sounds, it rhymes thoughts. The second line of a Hebrew poem doesn't rhyme with the first like English poetry does. The second line restates and refines or completes the first thought. This technique is called parallelism.

Psalm 34:3 is one example of it. It says, "Oh, magnify the Lord with me, and let us exalt his name together!" The first thought ("magnify the Lord with me") is parallel to the second ("let us exalt his name together"). Thus, the thoughts rhyme.

When God's thoughts and my thoughts are parallel with each other, I have peace—which is one of the fruits of the Spirit. It is like our thoughts are moving in the same direction in a coordinated fashion. But when my thoughts and God's thoughts are not moving in the same direction, it creates dissonance. I lose my peace. I may feel like God is not happy to see me or like it is pointless to seek Him because I don't feel like I'll get an answer. Peace is not the only test of whether a thought is from God, but it is part of the process.

Other tests include Scripture coming to life, the message conforming to Scripture, and the message producing the fruit of the Spirit. There are even tests you can do to directly challenge the source of a supernatural experience. I usually call this "if" prayers. They work like this. I pray, "If this experience is from the God who raised Jesus from the dead, then I thank Him for it and ask Him to help me use it for His glory. But if I have been deceived and this experience is a counterfeit from the devil, I renounce it and in the name of Jesus command that wicked spirit to leave." I have seen this prayer both confirm God's supernatural work and expose the deceptions of the adversary.

In my experience, most of the time we hear God's voice it is a right-brain experience. If we only ever listen for surprising, clear, distinct thoughts in the left side of our brains, we may think God does not often speak to us. However, once we realize that much of God's communication is nonverbal, it opens the door to sensing His presence more often.

GRATITUDE

The Bible regularly encourages us to give thanks to the Lord. I used to see this as a call to make checklists. I would pray things like, "God, thank you for my wife, for my family, for a pretty day," etc. It didn't create a tremendous amount of gratitude in my heart. I was just going through the motions and discharging a duty.

Once, when I was struggling with despair and feeling defeated, I opened my Bible to Psalm 107:1, which says, "Oh give thanks to the LORD, for he is good, for his steadfast love endures forever!" My first thought when I read this verse was accusatory. The thought said, "That is your problem. You are ungrateful." (Who does that sound like? Satan is the accuser.)

I then stopped and started my usual practice of making a list of good things in my life without taking the time to feel anything about them. Then I had another thought. This one said, "Read the verse again."

As I reread the verse, it jumped out at me that it didn't say to make a list of blessings. It specifically said to give thanks to God for His goodness and love. I realized that this was a God thought. I felt inspired to get a piece of paper and draw a diagram. It looked like this.

GOD

Goodness (*tov*)   **Love (*hesed*)**

Problems

ME

God wasn't speaking to me in clear, distinct words, but I could tell I was thinking with God. He was letting me know that I could thank Him in the midst of my problems because He was looking at me through eyes of goodness and love. He was already making plans to deal with every problem that were motivated by His goodness to me and His love.

I also recognized the word *love* as the Hebrew word *hesed*.[4] It specifically referred to the type of family attachment that communicated, "I will do good to you simply because you are mine." For example, the first use of *hesed* in the Bible has Abraham's servant asking Rebekah's family to let her leave them and marry Isaac (Gen. 24:12, 49). In his appeal, he basically says, "Are you going to show me *hesed*, or not?" In other words, are you going to do right by me as a family member or not?

As I pondered these things, I felt my spirits lift. Although I had not heard God distinctly or directly, it seemed clear that I had heard from God. I had spent enough years meditating on and memorizing Scripture to know that my thinking aligned with Scripture. So, by faith, I prayed,

> **When gratitude becomes a spirit of appreciation, and we feel the thankfulness for more than a few seconds, it prepares our hearts for connection with God.**

"Thank You, Father, for Your goodness and love. Thank You that I know I can count on You to take care of me because I am part of Your family, and You love me."

I then began going through my problems and saying, "Thank You that you have a good plan for dealing with this. Thank You that You have a loving plan for dealing with that. Thank You that I do not need to know what Your plans are, I just need to know that You are good and full of *hesed*."

When gratitude is simply a duty, we discharge it by making a list and checking off boxes. It doesn't accomplish much. But when gratitude becomes a spirit of appreciation, and we allow ourselves to feel the thankfulness for more than a few seconds, it prepares our hearts for connection with God. I think this is one of the reasons we are so often encouraged to enter God's presence with gratitude and praise. It isn't an obligation so much as an invitation to come relationally ready to meet with someone we enjoy.

PRAYER MODELS

Many people use different prayer patterns to guide them in connecting with God. I want to share a few that I have found helpful.

Doctrinal Prayer

Dr. Mark Bubeck wrote a pamphlet called *Prayer Patterns for Revival* that contains several examples of doctrinal prayers.[5] Dr. Bubeck was the founder of the ministry I lead and a great prayer warrior. He was a prayer partner to many of the great evangelical leaders of the last generation.

A doctrinal prayer is essentially a prayer written by someone else that we can read and make our own. It is a way of being mentored by someone who has sound theology and great experience with prayer. Mark's daughter Judy Dunagan also has a book that highlights the use of doctrinal prayer called *The Loudest Roar*.[6]

Listening for God's Agenda

Dr. Neil T. Anderson wrote a book called *Liberating Prayer*, in which he describes how his prayer life was transformed with one simple change.[7]

When Dr. Anderson was a pastor, he struggled with his prayer life for years. Studying the Bible was easy for him, but he never seemed to be able to engage in prayer for more than five to ten minutes. He heard stories about people who had refreshing and engaging times in prayer that lasted an hour or more and wondered what they were doing all that time.

Then, one night when he was preparing to teach on prayer, it occurred to him that in the Steps to Freedom in Christ (which we discussed in chapters 4 and 5), he encouraged people to ask God questions and then pay attention to the thoughts they had. He decided to try that with his personal prayer life.

After beginning with devotional reading and worship, he asked God, "Where do you want to start? What should I talk to you about first?" After he asked that question, whatever thought entered his mind guided him in prayer. In a sense, he was letting God create his prayer list. He often used a spiral notebook to write down the thoughts that came to mind and how he prayed about them.

Dr. Anderson noticed that he often got thoughts that were either clearly not from God or unrelated to prayer. Sometimes he had thoughts like, "This is stupid. What if you get deceived? You will never be any good at this." Such condemning thoughts were clearly targeted at getting him not to pray. He realized these were from the enemy, so he wrote them in a spiral notebook and rejected them. However, by writing them down, he noticed a pattern of enemy attacks, which helped him overcome those thoughts more quickly.

He also had thoughts like, "Don't forget to mow the lawn or change the oil." He also wrote those on a separate piece of paper. In a talk I heard him give, he said he often finished his prayer time with a "to-do list" completed as well.

Letting God set the agenda for his prayer life transformed Dr. Anderson's approach to prayer, and I have found it to be very effective in my own prayer time as well.

A LESSON FROM TOZER

Whichever prayer pattern you use, developing a conversational prayer life is an important part of learning to walk in the Spirit. In his classic book *The Pursuit of God*, A.W. Tozer wrote the following prayer:

> Lord, teach me to listen. The times are noisy and my ears are weary with the thousand raucous sounds which continuously assault them. Give me the spirit of the boy Samuel when he said to Thee, "Speak, for Thy servant heareth." Let me hear Thee speaking in my heart. Let me get used to the sound of Thy voice, that its tones may be familiar when the sounds of earth die away and the only sound will be the music of Thy speaking voice. Amen.[8]

Developing a conversational prayer life is an important part of learning to walk in the Spirit.

Every time I read Tozer's words, "the times are noisy and my ears are weary with the thousand raucous sounds which continually assault them," I am reminded of the fact that he ministered primarily from the 1920s to the 1950s. There was no TV for most of that time and no internet, yet it was still a challenge to stop and listen. Even so, there is no substitute for building our attachment to God than hearing His voice and sensing His guidance in our hearts.

FINAL THOUGHTS

If our identity in Christ is the foundation of the Christian life, then walking in the Spirit is the engine that runs it. Trying to live the Christian life in the flesh is a bit like a Jedi going into a fight and deciding not to use the Force. The reality is that New Age practitioners often do a better job of recognizing the necessity of the spirit world than Christians. Many of us function as if the Spirit world (demons, angels, or the Holy Spirit) is an afterthought. But one of the core concepts of the kingdom is that we are but branches attached to the vine (John 15:1–8). On our own, we can bear no fruit. The fruit God desires comes from walking in the Spirit. The more we grow in our capacity to recognize the Spirit's guidance, the easier this gets.

We have emphasized two main ideas on what it means to walk in the Spirit: Scripture and Spirit. In the New Testament, the group best known for their focus on Scripture without the Spirit were the Pharisees. These religious leaders were so focused on the objective that they could not be persuaded to recognize the Holy Spirit's work that was happening through the ministry of Jesus. No miracle or teaching of Jesus could open their eyes to the work of the Spirit.

In the same way, the Bible without the Spirit is not a recipe for success in the Christian life for us today. Throughout history, there have also been groups that got so focused on hearing God's voice experientially that they stopped caring if it was biblical. I have a friend whose wife divorced him and married someone else because the pastor at her church got a "word from the Lord" that she was supposed to disobey Scripture. People can fall into serious error on either extreme, which is why we need to walk in balance, as we talked about in the last chapter.

As you grow in biblical wisdom and focus on your walk with God today, I would encourage you to remember to SLOW down and take some time to connect with Him as you seek, listen, obey, and watch what happens.

CHAPTER 10

HEART-FOCUSED COMMUNITY

NOT LONG AGO, I RECEIVED a testimony from a woman who had been fully trained in traditional discipleship and devoted her life to discipling others but found she needed something deeper. She joined an online small group offered by Deeper Walk International called Journey Groups and wrote this testimonial:

> I have been a Christian for many years and was trained by [a very popular discipleship ministry]. I was very strong in spiritual disciplines and thought I was prepared to disciple others when I went to Europe as a missionary. After 17 years, I found out that my version of discipleship was not impacting lives in most cases, and I wondered what was missing.
>
> About 18 months ago, I joined a Journey Group online. My whole walk with God has been transformed as I have learned to increase my joy levels . . . my Christian life is no longer based on rowing (working hard, disciplines, pulling myself up by my bootstraps),

but I'm learning to sail (joyfully, cooperating with the Holy Spirit wherever He leads). Rowing is all based on hard work. Sailing is also work, but way more fun!! Also, I've learned that joy is contagious, and with COVID, politics, fires in California, hurricanes, riots, everyone needs more joy, even non-believers are eager to hear ways to increase their joy.[1]

This missionary offers a classic example of someone who had been fully discipled in half-brained Christianity. She knew a lot of truth. She did her best to be disciplined and make good choices. She sought God's power for ministry, and she had devoted her life to service.

So, what was missing? She was lacking relational joy.

Most of us don't think of joy when we think of discipleship. We think of hard work. We think of discipline—after all, isn't discipline embedded in the word itself? When we struggle, we think, "I need to get more serious about this." We don't think, "I need more joy." But the truth is, we grow best in an environment of joy.

If I am disconnected from community and isolated, my walk with God gets harder. It becomes more work. If I am in a toxic community that is actively sabotaging my joy, it can pull the rug out from under my efforts to grow. However, when I am in a community of people who are happy to be together and know how to handle emotions with maturity, it is hard not to grow.

THE OTHER HALF OF CHURCH

Nearly all discipleship ministries emphasize community, but most are still looking for the secret sauce that makes community work. In their book, *The Other Half of Church*, Michel Hendricks and Jim Wilder offer an answer to that problem.[2] They compare community to soil. Just as plants grow best in enriched soil, but can struggle or even die in distressed soil, so Christians grow best in healthy communities where there is a lot of relational joy.

Trying to grow plants in good soil is a completely different experience than trying to grow them in bad soil. My wife and I learned this the hard way. When we first planted a flower garden in front of our porch, a friend of ours who owned a farm brought over a load of cow manure and mixed it into the soil for us. Everything we planted that year grew strong and healthy with beautiful blooms. The next year, we skipped adding the manure. I was shocked at the difference. The exact same plants getting the same amount of sun and water struggled to survive because the soil was lacking the nutrients they needed in order to thrive.

Wilder and Hendricks identified four key elements of the kind of enriched soil that catalyzes growth:

1. Joy

In my own life, I think about the difference between the joy I felt as part of a vibrant youth ministry and the hopelessness I felt when I was isolated and alone in seminary. As part of the youth ministry, I was surrounded by people who really liked spending time together. I probably did something with members of this group four or five days a week. We invented reasons to spend time together. I don't think it is an accident that over thirty of us ended up in full-time ministry out of a youth group of 120 kids. We loved what we were experiencing and wanted to spend our lives spreading joy in the name of Christ.

Joy is a powerful catalyst for change. One of the core characteristics of the early church was the joy they shared in being together. In Acts 2:42–47, Luke paints a picture for us of a group of people who loved spending time together. They met together often and took care of each other's needs in a way that created "glad and generous hearts" (Acts 2:46).

2. Hesed

The Hebrew word *hesed* refers to a strong attachment that cares for others.[3] It embodies the kind of belonging that provides for and protects its people. When we belong to a group that takes care of one another, it creates a safety net for life. We know we will never have to go through anything alone. Our people will go through it with us. Knowing that we have strong, safe, and secure connections with our people creates an environment that makes growth almost automatic.

Perhaps you have been on a short-term missions trip to an impoverished country and noticed that the level of joy in the people was much higher than you would have expected. One of the reasons for this is that in most of these countries, people have deep family and deep church attachments. They are going through hard stuff, but they are going through it together and have learned how to be happy to be with each other in the midst of all the other big and difficult emotions.

3. Group Identity

As we discussed in an earlier chapter, my sense of identity is related to knowing who my people are. If I am a Republican and I read a headline trashing one of my people, it is easy to get angry before I even know what the details are and if there is any truth to the story. It is the same for Democrats or any other group I am attached to. I tend to want to defend my people. In fact, I will tend to dress like my people, talk like my people, believe like my people, and value what my people value. The desire to belong and be part of something has an energy of its own in shaping how I see myself and behave. The belonging and identity of being part of a group are some of the most powerful transformational forces on the planet.

Group identity is formed through belonging and vision. Jesus called His followers to leave behind their people and their attachments to this life and form a deep attachment to Him greater than all of the others. Becoming a follower of Christ gave everyone in the group a sense of identity. Each of them made sacrifices to belong. Their bond to each other was formed because they were all bonded to the same leader. The worldview and values that Jesus taught gradually became their worldview and values.

Paul continued this emphasis on building a strong group identity. Most of his letters followed a pattern of saying, "This is who we Christians are, and this is how it is like us to act."

When I can say, "These are my people," it means I feel like I belong to something bigger than myself that helps give my life purpose and me a sense of identity. This transformative power can be used for good or evil. Cults often excel at building a strong group identity. Most political action groups have a strong sense of belonging and vision that shapes the people in the group. In our journey toward a deeper walk with God, we need to learn how to harness the power of belonging to a group that is committed to the values of heart-focused discipleship.

4. Healthy Shame

No community is happy all the time. Every group must deal with disagreements and needs to correct behavior or attitudes that are out of line. We live in a culture that generally believes all shame is toxic, but this is not true. From a brain perspective, toxic shame is related to the narrative attached to the emotion. When the narrative is toxic, the shame becomes toxic. From a biblical perspective, healthy shame messages are called "rebukes" (Prov. 15:31; 2 Tim. 3:16). They are characterized by the ability to correct others in a way that keeps the relationship bigger than the problem.

In Revelation 3:19, Jesus says that He rebukes those He loves. It is a verse that is hard to translate into English. It uses the Greek word *philos* for love. This word carries with it the idea of friendship or deep attachment. Jesus is basically saying, "Because I love you like a brother (or a sister), I am going to correct what you are doing." As a parent, I get this. I correct my kids because I want what is best for them. I want them to get off of paths that I know will lead to heartache and even destruction. Because I love them, I want to guide them onto a different path. This can be done in a selfish way in which I really only care about myself— "Change what you are doing and stop making my life so difficult." Or, this can be done in a loving way that connects before correcting. In the same way, Christian communities need to learn how to keep relationships bigger than problems by starting and ending with the importance of the relationship and not just venting because there is a problem.

ELEMENTS OF A STRONG GROUP IDENTITY

On one level, it seems like nothing should be easier than "doing church." After all, we are gathering people together who love Jesus, are pledged to loving one another, and are committed to being salt and light in the world. What could go wrong? Apparently, everything.

From the very beginning, the church had relational problems. Ananias and Sapphira lied to the apostles to gain glory with their peers (Acts 5:1–11). A quarrel arose about the unjust treatment of foreign Christians (Acts 6:1). There were theological divisions that threatened to split the church (Acts 15; 1 Cor. 3:1–4). Nearly all of Paul's letters dealt with relational, moral, and theological problems in the churches he founded. There has never been any such thing as a perfect church.

One of the reasons churches struggle is the immaturity of our members. Another is that we have an enemy who is actively at work to sabotage the church. Jesus said the kingdom of heaven is like a man who planted a good crop, but that an enemy came in at night and planted weeds among the good seed (Matt. 13:24–30). In the same way, the apostle Paul warned against false apostles (2 Cor. 11:3; Rev. 2:2), false prophets (Matt. 24:11; 1 John 4:1), false teachers (2 Peter 2:1), and false believers (2 Cor. 11:26; Gal. 2:4). Upon leaving the elders of one church, he wept and warned them that "savage wolves" would rise up among them to devour the flock (Acts 20:29 NIV).

Faced with such challenges, it is informative to see how the apostles built spiritual families wherever they went that created such powerfully transformative identity groups, they "turned the world upside down" (Acts 17:6).

THE POWER OF WEAKNESS

At the heart of building a healthy group identity is how we view weakness. Predators prioritize staying at the top of the pecking order. They view weakness with disgust (whether in themselves or others) and see it as an opportunity to attack. In this sense, predators think like enemies. They want to hide their weaknesses, so they are less vulnerable to attack, and keep track of the weaknesses of others, so they know where to strike if they need to defend themselves from a perceived attack.

Healthy groups are run by protector leaders who are gentle with weakness. They don't view weakness with disgust. Instead, they see it as an opportunity for growth. The word *protector* fits such leaders because they stand up to bullies and predators, making it safe for those with weaknesses to grow.

Many of us need to learn how to show grace to ourselves as we deal with our weaknesses. Disgust, anger, and toxic shame are not healthy motivators, especially not over a long period of time. I may get disgusted with myself and vow to make changes, but that rarely lasts long. But when I learn that God is a gentle protector who helps me make changes out of His great love for me (and not out of His disgust or anger), I don't have to fear God's correction. I can welcome it.

The Necessity of Mature Leadership

The apostle Paul understood the purpose and importance of leadership. He made sure that churches had overseers (*episkopoi*). When he recognized that the Corinthian church was struggling to produce mature leaders, he sent Timothy to model what it meant to be a spiritual father (1 Cor. 4:17). When he listed the qualities necessary in a church leader, he did not focus on talent, training, and a track record of results. He focused on maturity (1 Tim. 3:2–7; Titus 1:5-9).

In our book *Rare Leadership in the Workplace*, Jim Wilder and I define *leadership* as "creating engagement in what matters."[4] Church leaders are called to build spiritual families. Too often, we have seen our task as building discipleship factories. The factory approach has merit, but it emphasizes programs and processes and counts on activities to generate growth. The family model focuses on emotional and relational maturity.

If you think back to chapter 1 for a moment, we looked at five levels of maturity development—infant, child, adult, parent, and elder. One of the biggest problems we have in discipleship is a lack of adults who model maturity, parents who can train others to be mature, and elders who bring maturity to the community as a whole.

Some of the common problems we see in our churches happen because maturity is either ignored or misidentified. Here are two examples of what I mean:

1. **Reverse maturity.** Reverse maturity (also called *upside-down maturity*)[5] happens when people essentially skip the child stage of development and start taking care of other people before they learn how to take care of themselves. If I become a leader because I am talented and experienced, I can find myself responsible for other people's growth without taking care of my own need for growth. The longer this goes on, the easier it is to hide the huge gap between what I know about the faith and how I actually live my life. The history of the church is littered with people who have looked great on Sunday in their positions of leadership but who hide secret sins and handle their families with anything but maturity.

   Reverse maturity is generally created when we miss the chance to be a child and have to parent our parents. Instead of learning how to take care of myself during the child stage of life, I am forced to take care of everyone else. As a result, I look very mature on the outside. I am usually a hard worker and very responsible. But I am generally stuck at child-level maturity when it comes to my emotions.

2. **Elder too soon.** One of the biggest mistakes churches make is making people elders too soon before they are actually at the stage of life to be an elder. In his book *The Complete Guide to Living with Men,*[6] Dr. Wilder devotes a chapter to the theme of the dangers of becoming an elder too soon. He offers many examples, but one that stood out to me was that of a leader who

led an international ministry for children while still raising his own kids. The problem wasn't that he was the leader. It was that he prioritized leading the ministry over his own family. He often said, "I'll take care of God's children, and God will take care of my children." But that is not how it works. While we are at the parent stage of life, parenting our children is priority one. The time for making the children of the world our priority comes later. In a sadly predictable story, this man's children became bitter. He lost his relationship with them, and they walked away from the faith. This is why becoming an elder too soon can often be catastrophic.

One of the reasons becoming an elder too soon is such a temptation is that it is easy to justify prioritizing the needs of the many ahead of the needs of the few. Far too many Christian leaders have fallen into this trap. When they have to choose between the good of the church and the good of their wives and children, the church always wins. But in the end, nobody wins.

Recently, the Christian world was rocked when a bestselling author announced on social media that he was done with Christianity. He was someone who had been placed on a pedestal in his twenties and prioritized ministry over his own family and his own walk with God. When the news hit, Jim Wilder sent me a short email that included the assessment, "This does seem like [a case of] an elder too soon."[7]

For a church to function as a healthy family, we need a lot of spiritual parents and elders. Part of the crisis in the church today is that we have so many spiritual infants and children playing the roles of parent and elder. It is a recipe for disaster, and the primary reason so many churches are a mile wide and an inch deep.

MORE VIBRANT SMALL GROUPS

As a former pastor, I know that a lot of Christian leaders have put a lot of thought and energy into how to build healthy communities. We are all looking for models to follow that have been successful somewhere else.

For the last several years, we have lived in a world of "plug and play" small groups in which leaders rarely receive any training, and there is no real agenda for the journey people are on. The result is that small groups often become the second parking lot for the church. We park people there and assume that they will grow without actually having a strategy for growth. I spoke with one small group pastor of a very large church who admitted that they didn't really care what people did in small groups. He just wanted to know they were connected. The idea was that if they were making relationships, they were going to be okay.

I'm sure most of us have been in great small groups. But I also think most of us have been in some rather bland if not dysfunctional small groups. So, what is it exactly that makes a small group vibrant and trans-formative? How do we create small groups with the transformational power we read about in our opening story?

Amy Brown is a relational skills trainer with a background in helping people with addiction recovery. Today, she's in leadership with an organization that trains people in listening prayer ministry called Alive & Well. We are good friends, and for a few years, she was on staff with Deeper Walk International.

We got connected when she attended an online training event I was leading and heard me say, "At some point, Deeper Walk needs to develop an online small group program."

She immediately contacted me and asked, "Do you know what I do?" I said no, and she went on to explain that she had already developed a basic curriculum for online small groups that was anchored in Jim Wilder's teachings. That got my attention.

It took about one day for our leadership team to offer her a position. That year, we launched the Deeper Walk Journey Group program and saw several hundred people participate. Stories of life change started flooding in.

We were a little skeptical about whether transformational community could be achieved online, but the results have been outstanding. So, is there a secret to the success of these groups? I think so. There are at least three core principles that make these groups so effective.

Check-Ins

Each session begins with an emotional "check-in." People get two minutes to tell others what emotions they are feeling as they come to the group that day. Some are joyful and excited, but others are struggling. Checking in this way gives everyone a chance to feel seen. We don't try to fix their problems. Now and then, we will pause to pray for someone if there is a specific problem and they want prayer. Most of the time, we just validate the emotion and let them know how glad we are that they have come. By beginning each meeting with authenticity and vulnerability, an environment of heart-to-heart connection is made possible. It is only in an environment that encourages us to let people see "the real me" that genuine connection can happen.

Curriculum

Journey Groups have a unique curriculum created by Amy Brown.[8] It is biblically based and focuses on the development of emotional maturity. It also includes the FISH model taught in this book. However, we encourage people to use this model with other curricula as well.

Listening Prayer

At the end of each session, the leader walks people through a time of listening prayer and journaling, then invites anyone who wants to share to read their journaling to the group for feedback. This only takes about ten to fifteen minutes. One of our leaders called this time of quieting, hearing, and sharing "the secret sauce" that makes Journey Groups so helpful.

When we pour out our struggles to God in the listening prayer time, and write down the thoughts that come to mind from God back to us, it lets others in the group "see" into our heart (because we were honest in our journaling to God), and also lets them see facets of God's heart (which they may not have seen before) because they are hearing us read our impressions of what God put on our heart in response to our journaling.

Imagine the impact on a church if our small group leaders received the kind of training that helped them experience whole-brained, heart-focused discipleship? It could revolutionize the church.

START WHERE YOU ARE

As we look to go deeper in our walk with God, it is important to realize that this isn't all about self-discipline, solitude, and study. While those things matter, it is just as vital to have the right kind of soil. To accomplish this, we need a multi-generational community. That means a community that has everyone from elders to infants involved. If you feel like you can't find a single church with all of that, it is okay. Start where you are. You don't have to start with all the pieces in place. Here are some suggestions:

1. Join a group and find a way to add value.
2. Look for ways to spread joy in small doses to the people who are already in your life.
3. Keep an eye out for people who have a similar heart for growth.
4. Don't expect to be best friends with people quickly. Trust has to be built one level at a time.
5. Pray that God will bring just the right people into your life and help you recognize them.

Not everyone reading this book is at the same level of maturity. Some are infants looking for someone to take care of them because they are overwhelmed. Some are children who can take care of themselves or someone else but not two people at the same time. Others are adults, parents, or elders who have the skills to begin creating community wherever they go.

Your next steps will largely depend on where you are in your personal development, and that is okay. The goal is to keep taking steps toward the next level of maturity.

CHAPTER 11

MISSION

FOR MOST OF MY LIFE, I was taught that Christians had an obligation to be a witness and to explain the gospel to people. Far too often, that message was motivated by shame. I remember being ten years old when a pastor's sermon convinced me that if I were really a good Christian, I would find a way to tell other people about Jesus every day.

I took him seriously. I left church that night and went straight to my friend's house. I had no idea what I was doing. I just knew it was my job to witness.

He answered the door, and I asked him, "Are you a Christian?"

He said, "Well, I'm Catholic."

I looked at him and said, "I don't think that is the same thing." He wasn't sure either. (Clearly, we had two astute theologians locked in deep debate.)

Suddenly, I realized I was at the end of my training, so we dropped the subject and moved on to something else.

Later, when I was in high school, something similar happened. I became convicted during a sermon that good Christians lead other people to Christ, so I invited a friend from the basketball team to get together.

I told him that I thought most people who really understood the gospel would want to receive Jesus. He agreed to listen to what I had to say, which is when I panicked. I suddenly realized I had no game plan for what to say.

My friend had come to have fun and spend time together, not get a sales pitch anchored in the reality of demons. But I found myself talking about them and how knowing they were real and that Christians had authority over them had convinced me that God was real. I got about that far and realized I was digging myself a hole I didn't know how to climb out of.

Once again, I dropped the subject. I was so embarrassed, and my friend felt so awkward that we really didn't hang out much after that.

You can read these stories and think my problem was a lack of training, and you would be partially right. But there was a deeper problem: I was sharing the gospel out of shame, trying to make sure God was happy with me. My approach to evangelism came from a fear bond with God rather than the overflow of the joy I experienced in my relationship with Him.

While our joy matters, the purpose of a whole-brained, heart-focused approach to discipleship is not only to grow our happiness but to equip us to impact the world with the same gospel that has changed and is changing us. Heart-focused discipleship also helps us understand that evangelism is not a stand-alone activity isolated from the rest of discipleship. It is an essential part of the task of presenting "everyone mature in Christ" (Col. 1:28).

I once taught a sermon on the kingdom of God in which I summed up the core values of the kingdom with these words:

- **Salvation**—Nothing is more important than entering the kingdom.
- **Stewardship**—Eternal rewards far outweigh earthly praise.

- **Spirituality**—Apart from Christ we can do nothing; all things are possible with Him.
- **Servant Love**—The mark of the Christian is loving others as Jesus (who washed the disciples' feet) loved us.

From these core values, it is not hard to see that mission is a high priority for the kingdom. We want people to be saved. *Check.* We want to steward what God has entrusted to us for the advancement of the kingdom. *Check.* We do all of this while relying on the wisdom and power of the Holy Spirit. *Check.* As we go on mission, we lead with love. *Check.* All of these core values are related to the mission of taking the gospel to others. It is not all they are about, but there is a clear connection.

In this chapter, I want to focus on how the FISH model—freedom, identity, Spirit, and heart-focused community—can help us understand and engage in the mission of the church. The word evangelism comes from the word *evangelium,* which is Latin for the gospel. Since the FISH model is anchored in the gospel, it makes sense that each of these elements would play a role in spreading the gospel to others.

FREEDOM

An experienced pastor with a doctoral degree in apologetics felt called to France as a missionary. It was the late 1980s, and he went to Europe fully expecting to have intellectual debates with Enlightenment-trained atheists about the evidence for Christianity. But Europe had already moved past that stage and was mostly postmodern when he arrived. They weren't really interested in debating what was true. They were mainly disinterested in the Christian idea of truth. He didn't lead a single person to Christ in his first term.

During his furlough, he spent time with my father and learned about spiritual warfare. He dealt with issues in his own life and discussed the role of warfare in spreading the gospel. When he returned to

France, he started talking to people about spirituality and power. Suddenly, they were interested.

Most of them followed their horoscopes faithfully, and occult spirituality was everywhere. A few people who were in emotional and behavioral bondage came to see him, and he was able to help them get free from their demons. Suddenly, their interest in truth increased. That term, he led several people to Christ and started a small church. Helping people find freedom had been the launching point for his ministry.

A friend named Randy, who lives in Kentucky, helped build a freedom ministry in his home church. For over two years, the church never had a Sunday go by without at least two people giving their lives to Christ. It wasn't uncommon to see fifty new converts in a week. The church was very seeker-driven. They had the full light show, professional-caliber music, and relevant preaching. But that wasn't the whole story.

The church also had one of the most active recovery ministries in the region. Hundreds of people gathered every week to work on their addictions and baggage. As a core part of this ministry, Randy used training material our ministry had developed to equip over fifty people in the basics of spiritual warfare ministry. Through his influence, I was a frequent guest speaker at this group. So many people were growing in freedom and telling others where to find help that hundreds of people were coming to Christ just through the recovery ministry.

At one point, Randy told me it had been over a year since a week had gone by when he had not personally had to help someone from the church get free from demonic strongholds. Here is a quick story of the kind of stuff that was happening.

A teenage girl had a severe medical issue. She was involuntarily vomiting about twenty times every day. She had been to several major medical clinics and seen a variety of specialists. She was on her way to Indianapolis to look into a surgery that would implant a device into her stomach when she and her mom stopped by the church to meet with the prayer team.

Randy was there and asked if they were okay with him checking to see if spiritual warfare was involved. It didn't take long before two demons identified themselves. One was there because of ancestral anorexia in the family. The other was there because of fear. He led the girl to renounce the permission they had been given and in using her authority to command the demons to leave. Her problem was instantly resolved. A few months later, she felt the impulse to vomit involuntarily and called for help. Randy assured her they were just testing to see if she would let them back in and to command them to leave. It worked, and she has been living in freedom from this torment for many years.

It is easy to miss the connection between helping people find freedom and doing the work of evangelism. It is not usually the first strategy people think of when they contemplate missions. But if we go back to the foundation of Christ's ministry, we find that freedom was right at the heart of it. In Luke 4:18–19, we read what many have called Christ's kingdom manifesto. It says:

The Spirit of the Lord is on Me,
because He has anointed Me
to preach good news to the poor.
He has sent Me
to proclaim *freedom* to the captives
and recovery of sight to the blind,
to *set free* the oppressed,
to proclaim the year of the Lord's favor. (HCSB, emphasis added)

The apostle John summed up Christ's mission with these words, "The reason the Son of God appeared was to destroy the works of the devil" (1 John 3:8). Just as freedom was core to the mission of Christ, so it must be core to the mission of the church. A well-functioning freedom ministry creates a natural flow of helping new believers find healing and deliverance who then tell others about the new freedom they have found.

IDENTITY

I had a friend in seminary who wanted to be a missionary to a country where Christians were persecuted. We had this conversation during the early 1990s, and this area was under a very oppressive Communist regime.

When I asked my friend why he wanted to go to this country, he said, "I've heard it is the hardest place on earth to be a missionary." As I pushed in a little more, he confessed he thought God would only be happy with him if he did the hardest work possible.

It became clear my friend thought he had to perform to be loved. He was going into missions hoping to earn God's love. That's not a healthy foundation. Instead of entering ministry out of an identity anchored in God's love, he was hoping to feel loved by going into ministry. By the time we were done talking, he had a new perspective. He had recently been introduced to materials on grace and his identity in Christ. He had just missed the connection to his plans. In the end, he got married, stayed in the States, and volunteered at a church ministering to the ethnic group he had felt called to serve.

My dad told me of a young lady on assignment in South America who was struggling with her emotions and about to leave the mission field. As they talked, he realized that no one had ever explained to her the basics of who she was in Christ.

When he told her that from God's perspective, she was a member of the royal family of the universe and that God thought of her as a princess, she began to cry. The thought was overwhelming to her.

She had spent her whole life feeling worthless and had hoped that giving her life away in ministry would give her value. Understanding her identity in Christ gave her a new foundation for ministry. Value was not something she could earn through hard work. Instead, her value was embedded in her identity as a deeply loved daughter of God.

Not only does understanding your identity in Christ provide the proper foundation for mission, but it is an important part of what we invite people to experience when we share Christ. As a pastor, I had a lot of people from outside of the church make appointments to see me because I had a reputation for being able to help with emotional healing. These sessions often led to opportunities to share the gospel with people.

As I mentioned in chapter 3, I got into the habit of starting with the bridge diagram and how we could not reach God through our effort, so God built a bridge to us in Christ. But I also put a question mark on the other side of the bridge and asked, "What happens when you say yes to Jesus? What changes? Do you simply get forgiveness and eternal life, or is there something more?" Very few of them had any idea where this was going.

I would use the opportunity to explain their identity in Christ. It usually went something like this.

Imagine that after you cross the bridge, you are greeted by a heavenly lawyer (and no, that is not an oxymoron). The lawyer says he needs to go over some paperwork with you.

Document number one is your pardon. It grants you forgiveness for all of your sins, the deposit of the righteousness of Christ into your account, and gives you eternal life. That is pretty great, isn't it? But there is more.

Document number two is your adoption papers. You are made a member of the royal family and granted an inheritance as part of the family. It gives you access to God, authority to represent the family (which is why we can pray in the name of Jesus and serve as ambassadors of the kingdom), and the deep assurance that you are loved and chosen.

Document number three is your citizenship papers. Crossing the bridge means you are dying to your identity as a citizen of this world and you are becoming a citizen of the kingdom of heaven. This document makes you a stranger and an alien in this world, since your home and people are now defined by the kingdom of God.

After reviewing these legal documents with you, he tells you to kneel down. He takes out a sword and taps you on each shoulder. He declares that you are now a saint. You are more than a sinner saved by grace—you have become a saint. In all of these ways, God gives you a new identity in Christ as the foundation of a whole new life.

Your meeting with the heavenly lawyer establishes a new legal foundation for your life. What happens next brings all of those legal realities to life:

- You are filled with the Holy Spirit so you can have a personal relationship with God. He will live in you and be with you.
- You can learn to talk to Him, listen to Him, and live with the wisdom and power He gives you.
- You are also brought into a community of believers who share the same identity and the same Spirit. You don't go through life alone. You go through life with other broken people who have recognized their utter dependence on God and the amazing gift of salvation that is ours in Christ.

After sharing all of this, I asked, "Does this sound like something you want?" They all had the same reaction. They knew they needed Jesus, but they had no idea all of this was part of the package. Every one of them entered into a covenant relationship with Christ and started their journey with enthusiasm at all God had done for them.

SPIRIT

If we are walking in the Spirit and growing in our relationship with Him, we can count on the fact that He will lead us into greater kingdom impact. Learning to sense when God is opening doors and pay attention when He calls us to act will inevitably open the door to mission.

Lee Strobel, a Christian who worked as a journalist for the *Chicago Tribune*, loves to tell people about Jesus. He is a bestselling author on apologetics and a former atheist who had set out to prove Christianity was false only to surrender fully to Christ.[1]

Early in his days as a Christian, Lee was learning to pay attention to the Spirit's voice. One day, he felt led to invite his atheist coworker to church. It was nearly Easter, and with such a clear prompting from the Spirit, he thought, "This is great! If God is prompting me to do this, something wonderful is probably going to happen. He's probably going to repent right there."[2]

Lee entered the office with a tremendous amount of confidence. However, his coworker shut him down completely. He finally said, "I don't want to go to your stupid church."

Lee was confused. However, several years later, he learned the rest of the story.

A man approached him after preaching one Sunday and thanked him for the influence he had made on his life. It turns out that he was in the coworker's office on the day Lee felt prompted to share Christ and invite his friend to church.

The man said, "You started talking to this guy about God, and you started inviting him to your church, and you gave the evidence that Jesus rose from the dead, and this guy was shutting you down. I'm on my hands and knees working this tile, listening to all this, and I'm thinking, 'I need God.'"

As Lee left the office in confusion, this man left the office and called his wife to tell her they were going to church that Easter. The Spirit's guidance suddenly made sense. God's ways are not our ways.

I heard Lee share this story many years ago, and he referred to the event as "ricochet evangelism."[3] He shared the gospel with one person, but it bounced off him and hit someone else. The story has stuck with me as a prime example of what it looks like to follow the Spirit's leading in the way we engage in outreach.

I experienced the Spirit's leading in evangelism early in my marriage. My wife Brenda and I lived in Texas. We were praying for our neighbors and asking God to open a door for salvation in their lives.

One Sunday night, Brenda told me she had arranged for us to go out for dinner with them. You would think I would have been delighted. After all, we had been praying for an open door. But I was tired. I had to get up early for work the next morning. I just wanted to relax and go to bed early. I left the house to run an errand feeling grumpy and upset with Brenda for making a plan without me.

Just a few minutes into the drive, I sensed the Holy Spirit speaking to me. "You are just feeling sorry for yourself. Haven't you been praying for an opportunity like this? Throwing a pity party really isn't going to help." The thoughts were surprising and out of line with what I had been thinking. But I knew they were right.

I came home, apologized for my attitude, and we all went out to dinner. It turned out to be an enjoyable evening and launched a relationship in which we had many spiritual conversations with our friends who we learned had been deeply wounded by the church. God didn't use us to lead them to Christ, but we supplied a bridge that made Christianity more appealing to them.

As we read the book of Acts, it becomes evident that the mission of the church was driven by the Holy Spirit. The disciples were told to wait for the outpouring of the Spirit before they did anything. The Spirit enabled the apostles to perform many miracles, the Spirit orchestrated events that opened doors for the gospel, and the Spirit confirmed the gospel message to those who believed.

In many parts of the world today, the role of the Spirit in evangelism is dramatic. My wife and I had friends who converted to Christianity after Jesus appeared to each of them in a series of visions in their Middle Eastern country. These appearances have become so common that someone told me there was a billboard in one country with a picture of Jesus on it that said, "If you have seen this person in a dream, call us."

My friend and pastor, Woody Cumbie, often traveled to the Middle East to do leadership training. At one such event, he overheard pastors having a theological conversation. It seems that nearly all of them had become Christians when Jesus had healed either them or a member of their family. They had assumed that Jesus would therefore heal every disease and sickness that came their way.

However, that was not their experience. Universally, they had found that such miracles only seemed to happen in evangelistic settings. Clearly, they did not lack the faith to be healed. They came fully expecting that this was the norm.

I'm not sure where they landed with their theology, but isn't it interesting that the Spirit was operating just as He had in the book of Acts? Miracles, signs, and wonders were driving the spread of the gospel. Our challenge is learning how to keep in step with the Spirit, not convincing Him to do what we think He should do.

HEART-FOCUSED COMMUNITY

In the last chapter, we said that community is like the soil in which people grow. The more vibrant and richer our community, the easier it is to develop maturity. The same can be said for evangelism and outreach. This is true in at least two ways:

1. When I am part of a healthy group, I know that I will never have to go through anything alone. This gives me greater capacity to take risks for God.
2. When I know that I can invite people to a group where they will be helped to find freedom, grounded in their identity in Christ, and trained to live in the Spirit, it is natural to want to invite people to share the experience.

When I was a pastor, a woman from the congregation asked to meet with me. She wanted to talk about addiction recovery because she was a mental health professional, and that was her area of expertise.

Partway through the conversation, she said, "You do know that this church has a reputation in the community for being the AA (Alcoholics Anonymous) church in the area. You may not realize it, but a lot of the people who have gravitated to the church attend AA meetings regularly."

I took that as a compliment. It meant they felt safe here. They felt like it was a community that would help them on their journey. It also meant they were telling other people that they had found a church where they were accepted.

One of the tragedies I often see in churches is the enormous gap between the leadership culture, the congregational culture, and the recovery culture. One church comes to mind as especially instructive. Their recovery ministry was fantastic. People were coming to Christ regularly and creating a culture of authenticity that discouraged wearing emotional and spiritual masks. People were encouraged not to pretend to be something they were not. Close friendships were formed, and it functioned almost like a church within the church.

However, in the leadership circles of the church, this was not the case. Narcissism reigned in the inner circles of church power. Masks were firmly in place. Everyone had learned to walk on eggshells around a temperamental but gifted leader.

Can you guess what happened? The church eventually split. The narcissist got caught in an affair, and the entire infrastructure of the church imploded. The one constant through it all was the recovery ministry, where people had learned to share each other's burdens and operate with transparency and grace. The stability of this group and the leaders who shared their values allowed the church to rebuild, but there are two important lessons to be learned.

1. We Need to Practice Transparency

People need to know we have weaknesses. Nobody wins when we pretend we have it all together. Heart-focused communities are characterized by transparency. The strong members of the group use their strength to help the weak, not ignore them. If people learn that sharing their weakness will get them in trouble, they learn to wear masks and hide what they fear is unacceptable to others. This is a big problem because people who conceal their weaknesses can't grow.

None of us can afford to live our lives in isolation or keep a part of our lives hidden so that no one knows about it. We all need people in our lives who are at parent- or elder-level maturity to whom we can bring our weaknesses. We don't necessarily open up to everyone we meet with the darkest secrets in our hearts because some people can be predatory with that kind of information. But we need to find people with whom we can take off our masks and be transparent.

2. We Need to Focus on Maturity Development

The goal of heart-focused discipleship is to help people move from one stage of maturity to the next. When this happens, churches tend to grow. However, when we prioritize church growth over maturity development, we can sabotage the success of our outreach. If people are growing in maturity and their lives are better because of their connection to the group, they will naturally invite others to join. However, churches that focus on growing in size rather than depth tend to fall into a trap. They attract a lot of people with the excellence of their programs, which generates a lot of energy and excitement. But if people attend the church for two or three years and don't feel like they are growing because a heart-focused community has not been developed, those people will start to leave.

Once a church has lost more people than currently attend, it is very hard to turn that around. The best way I know to change the church's reputation in the community is by becoming a place that routinely helps people move to the next stage of maturity.

I am not opposed to church growth or being creative in finding ways to grow. I am all for it. This is mostly a matter of priorities. A family that keeps making babies but never trains them in maturity is going to have a disaster on its hands. It is the same with churches. We don't win people to Christ simply to add to the number of people who attend or to be able to say we have led 10,000 people to Christ. We do it knowing that our community is organized and trained to lead those people to maturity.

KINGDOM IMPACT

Mission encompasses everything that goes into taking back ground from the enemy and preparing a bride for Christ. One of the goals of heart-focused discipleship is to equip people to make an impact for the kingdom. To do this, we need to be Spirit-led and growing in our maturity. We don't have to be perfect to have an impact. We simply need to be obedient to what God asks of us. The deeper we grow in our walk with Him, the more natural it will be to sense His leading situation by situation.

God has made each of us unique and given us different passions and gifts. How we go about spreading the gospel is less about the method and more about staying in step with the Spirit. By staying engaged in the process of heart-focused discipleship, we put ourselves in the best position to sense God's leading.

In the end, it is not our job to make an impact. That is God's job. Our job is to be obedient to what He calls us to do. As the apostle Paul wrote, "I planted, Apollos watered, but God gave the growth" (1 Cor. 3:6). You never know what small act of kindness God will use to make an enormous difference in the world.

I often marvel at how God sometimes touches people, ministries, books, or seemingly random actions and uses them to accomplish something extraordinary. I was at a conference a few years ago, standing at a booth where we were selling resources and providing information about our ministry. Someone stopped by and the Lord prompted me to give him a booklet I had written called *REAL Prayer*.[4] It provided a quick explanation of the prayer process I talked about in chapter four that I often used when leading people to connect with God regarding past wounds.

The next day I got an email from the man telling me he had read the booklet at a rest stop on the drive home, prayed through the prayer pattern, and experienced something miraculous. As he revisited an old memory, God took away the pain and gave him a new perspective. He just wrote to say thank you.

When I gave him the booklet, I had no idea if he would even read it. I didn't know if he needed it or not. But God took that small seed and used it to accomplish something profound in this man's life. I am guessing you have similar stories—times when a small act of obedience led to real impact.

Even if you are a spiritual infant just starting on the journey, you have something someone needs. It might be your story. It might be a word of encouragement or an act of kindness. If you are farther down the path, God may be calling you to step up and join a team. He may even be calling you to start something new. As we mature in our walk with God, He sometimes calls us to bigger roles, but He also sometimes calls us to more private roles. Many of the most devoted intercessors I know are spiritual elders. They are not well known and do not lead large ministries, but they have tremendous kingdom impact through prayer.

Wherever you are at in your maturity development, you can make an impact for the kingdom. As we are faithful to what God has called us to do, He will take care of the results.

EPILOGUE

ONE OF THE PRIMARY OBJECTIVES of this book has been to set forth a clear path to a deeper walk with God. The goal of this process is to move from infant- to child- to adult-level maturity and then grow into becoming spiritual parents who mentor others and spiritual elders who oversee the community and take younger Christians under their wing. The path itself is built on the five core elements of the gospel:

- **Freedom**—If you want to go deeper in your walk with God, you need to include emotional healing and spiritual warfare as part of your journey. It is impossible to run the race set before us if we are weighed down with rocks and tied up with ropes.
- **Identity**—Maturity can be measured by our ability to act like ourselves even when we are experiencing hardship. Understanding who we are in Christ and seeing the unique heart values God has given each of us is the foundation on which a deeper walk is built.

- **Spirit**—A deeper walk is primarily characterized by living in the Spirit. We cannot hope to bear the fruit that characterizes mature Christianity apart from a deep dive into Scripture and learning to recognize the voice of God.
- **Heart-focused community**—Just as a plant needs nutrient-rich soil in order to flourish, so we need a multi-generational, heart-focused community in order to develop a vibrant walk with God.
- **Mission**—Being salt and light in the world doesn't start with shame and guilt. It flows out of freedom, identity, walking in the Spirit, and the experience of joyful community. Kingdom impact is about inviting people to experience the new life offered in the gospel.

As you seek a more vibrant walk with God, this is the path you need to take. It is not a path to perfection. It is not a path to problem-free living. It is a path that goes deeper in faith, deeper in obedience, and leads to more fearless living. These are not destinations we can simply choose to experience. They are capacities we must work to grow.

May you find joy in the journey and hope for your souls as you follow this gospel path to a deeper walk with God.

SUMMARY OF MEMORY DEVICES

THE FIVE GOSPEL FOUNDATIONS

FREEDOM	We died with Christ in order to be free from bondage.	Discipleship should include spiritual warfare and emotional healing.
IDENTITY	We are raised with Christ in order to build on a new foundation.	Discipleship should train us to live out our new identity even when enduring hardship.
SPIRIT	We are born of the Spirit in order to walk in the Spirit.	Discipleship should train us in how we walk in the Spirit.

HEART-FOCUSED COMMUNITY	We are born into the family of God in order to love God and others well.	Discipleship should be anchored in heart-focused community.
MISSION	We are called to play our role in taking Christ to the world.	Discipleship should train us to move into mission.

VALUES OF A KINGDOM WORLDVIEW

SALVATION	Nothing is more important than entering the kingdom.
STEWARDSHIP	We must seek first God's kingdom and righteousness.
SPIRITUALITY	Only by abiding in Christ can we bear kingdom fruit.
SERVANT LOVE	The mark of the Christian is love.

COMMON MODEL OF WOUNDED HEARTS

WOUNDS	The world wounds us.	Plowed soil
LIES	The devil lies to us.	Seeds
VOWS	The flesh makes vows.	Vines
STRONGHOLDS	Strongholds are the result.	Unwanted fruit

WAYS WE OPEN DOORS TO THE DEVIL

SIN	Unconfessed sin of all sorts
OCCULT	Secret knowledge and power
UNFORGIVENESS	Not canceling debts
LIES WE BELIEVE	The devil's propaganda
LINEAGE	Generational consequences

HOW WE RECLAIM SURRENDERED GROUND*

CONFESS	Admit what opened the door
CANCEL	Repent, renounce, and forgive
COMMAND	Evict spirits
COMMIT	Dedicate to Christ

* Karl I. Payne, *Spiritual Warfare: Christians, Demonization, and Deliverance* (Alexandria, VA: Republic Book Publishers, 2011).

NEW COVENANT IDENTITY

PARDON	Justification, purification, redemption
ADOPTION	Access, authority, inheritance
CITIZENSHIP	Ambassadors
TITLE: SAINT	Holy ones—not of this world

BUILDING BLOCKS OF BIBLICAL THEOLOGY

Deeper Walk Guide to the Bible—www.PLAXN.com

WORSHIP	We were created to walk with God
WARFARE	We live in a world at war
WISDOM	Scripture and the Spirit give us light in the darkness
PROMISE	Abraham
LAW	Moses
ANOINTED ONE	David
EXILE	Jeremiah, Ezekiel, Daniel
NEW COVENANT	Jesus—the gospel
COMING OF MESSIAH	The coming kingdom

WALKING IN THE SPIRIT

SEEK (STOP)	Seek God—ask questions
LISTEN	Notice God thoughts
OBEY	Do what God directs
WATCH	Watch what happens

BIBLE MEMORIZATION TIPS

1. Memorization requires both creativity and repetition. Creativity sparks our emotions, and an emotional connection to the material is essential to remember it.

2. Set aside thirty minutes for memorization work at least four times each week.

3. Read one sentence or phrase at a time out loud three times. Then close your eyes and repeat that phrase. Repeat the process until you can say the phrase perfectly three times. Then move to the next line. Once you have recited that line three times, perfectly connect the two lines together and recite them. Once you can recite them perfectly twice, move to the third line. I have found that the average person can memorize three to five verses in fifteen minutes or less using this process. I have also discovered that most people forget everything they learned the next day because it is all in

short-term memory. That is okay. Expect it. Just relearn them the next day, and you will find the process goes much more quickly the second time. By the end of the week, you will want to recite everything you learned that week with a partner.

4. Pretend you are an actor on stage reciting your lines. Add blocking and inflection and points of emphasis as if you were giving a speech. Say some things slowly. Some quickly. Some with dramatic pauses inserted. The more creativity you add to the process, the more easily you will remember the lines.

5. Take walks as you memorize. I often tried to walk in different places with each chapter I worked on. One chapter would remind me of the baseball diamonds at the park. One would remind me of trails by the river. Another one of the neighborhood where a friend lived. For example, let's say you wanted to memorize Ephesians. It has six chapters. You could use your house and yard as memory tools. Your bedroom might be chapter 1. The upstairs rooms could be chapter 2, the living room chapter 3, the kitchen chapter 4, the front yard chapter 5, and the backyard chapter 6. These types of mental connections can aid memorization.

6. Find a partner. I found it absolutely essential that at least once a week, I met with someone willing to help me learn my lines as if I was an actor in a play. I just thought of it as "running lines."

ONE-YEAR TRANSFORMATION PLAN

FOR THOSE WHO ARE LOOKING for a simple plan to begin implementing heart-focused discipleship in their own life, here is a simple three-step strategy I would recommend:

1. Form a group and study this book together.
2. Schedule at least one freedom appointment (or have the people in your group practice with each other).
3. Create a Relational Rhythm with God
   - Daily
   - Weekly
   - Monthly
   - Seasonally

A MINISTRY MODEL

AT ONE POINT, when I was a pastor, our church had more people attending small groups throughout the week than attending our Sunday morning services. We basically ran the church through our small group ministry. We liked to say we were a church *of* small groups, not a church *with* small groups.

Our goal was to have a maturity development system in place that created a clear path for growth in the church. We called it the Life System, and it included life groups, life classes, and a life center. I will introduce it here as a possible ministry model for those looking to create a maturity development system in their church.

LIFE GROUPS

At the heart of the process were small groups we called life groups. Each group functioned with five core values:

1. **Socialize.** We wanted the groups to spend time doing things
   that created joy. This meant that small group times weren't the
   only times groups met. Sometimes two or three groups would
   have a picnic together or coordinate holiday activities.
2. **Serve.** We encouraged groups to serve in two primary ways.
   One, if someone got sick or went to the hospital, the small group
   members were the first responders who made sure they were
   looked after. Meals were provided, and a visitation schedule was
   created. Two, we asked groups to pick one service project every
   year that they could do as a group. Having seen the bonding that
   often occurred in short-term missions, we wanted to see people
   bonding over making life better for others.
3. **Study.** Groups rotated between curriculum the church leadership provided for them and studying materials of their choosing, but there was always a learning element to the groups. As
   you can imagine, we had a major stress on issues related to
   freedom, identity, Spirit, and heart-focused community.
4. **Stories.** One of the expectations was that everyone in the group
   got a chance to tell their story. An important part of belonging is
   knowing that people see you and understand something about
   your journey. Over time, these stories got more intimate. It was
   important for the leader to set a bar for what was the appropri-
   ate amount of transparency. Too little and people would feel like
   they had to wear masks. Too much and people would be scared
   off. Small groups are not recovery groups. It is a place for sharing
   authentic emotion, but not necessarily all of the details of one's
   failures. The primary reason for this is that not everyone has the
   capacity to deal with how dark life can get. This doesn't mean
   such conversations can't happen outside of group time. We just
   need to be careful to not overwhelm people.
5. **Prayer support.** We had a church-wide prayer initiative that
   made sure at least one person was fasting and praying for the
   church each day and assigned each small group a particular

week to come to the church to pray over the auditorium. One of the goals was to make sure that both individuals and ministries were always covered in prayer.

LIFE INSTITUTE

In addition to the small group ministry, we launched a Life Institute with three tracks of classes:

1. **Bible and theology.** We offered Bible survey courses, church history courses, and classes related to theology and apologetics. Our goal was to provide these in a variety of formats that could be accessed either in person or online.
2. **Ministry skills.** In this track, we covered issues like evangelism, spiritual gifts, freedom ministry, prayer ministry, and more.
3. **Life skills.** This track included courses related to care ministry topics like personal finances, addiction recovery, marriage and family, grief, and more.

We encouraged individuals to take at least three courses a year. Many of these classes were only a few hours or a day of content. Others required several weeks of participation. The idea is that people need content and training. Content happens best in a classroom setting. Training happens best through experience and mentoring.

LIFE CENTER

The third leg of the Life System was the development of a life center. This was basically the care ministry of the church. It was a place where people could schedule appointments to discuss personal issues or receive prayer ministry related to freedom and healing.

ACKNOWLEDGMENTS

BOOKS LIKE THIS really are a team effort. First, I would like to thank Duane Sherman for his consistent encouragement and willingness to talk through themes together. I also want to thank Ashleigh Slater, who did an outstanding job of taking what I wrote and making it better with hundreds (if not thousands) of suggestions, confirmations, and corrections. I also want to express my thanks to Nik Harrang, my friend and the Director of Operations at Deeper Walk, who took a weekend that was already full and not only made it through the entire manuscript, but offered a string of insightful pearls on how to make this book better and how to spell out the biblical foundations of some of the lessons more solidly.

Finally, I have dedicated this book to my dad. It is hard to overstate his influence in setting me on the path that made this book possible. You will see his name and his stories in many of the chapters. No one is perfect (I certainly am not) but it was an honor to be raised in the Warner family. Both my mom and my dad were deeply devoted to Christ in a way that made them want to be the best people possible. Theirs was never a story of looking good at church but behaving differently at home. When I struggled to make my faith my own as a teenager, one of the realities I could not refute was that what my parents had was real. I hope this book helps spread the reality of a deeper walk to more and more people. It is the best legacy I can imagine leaving in their honor.

NOTES

INTRODUCTION: MY STORY

1. A *power encounter* refers to a confrontation between the religious spirits worshiped by the local population and the Spirit of Christ. People have come to Christ all over the globe, not because of the logic of the Christian faith (though they later came to see that), but because the power of Christ was greater than the power of the gods they served.

CHAPTER 1: HALF-BRAINED CHRISTIANITY

1. Shared with the author during a small gathering of Christian leaders as part of a conversation on Christian counseling, 2004.
2. Cited from Marcus Warner, *Toward A Deeper Walk: Heart-Focused Training for the Journey of Life* (Carmel, IN: Deeper Walk International, 2012), 14–15.
3. Russ Rainey, "Summary of the Willow Creek REVEAL Study," *The Christian Coaching Center,* accessed February 18, 2022, http://www .christiancoachingcenter.org/index.php/russ-rainey/coachingchurch2/.
4. This is the same thesis as the one found in the title of Peter Scazzero's book, *Emotionally Healthy Spirituality: It's Impossible to be Spiritually Mature, While Remaining Emotionally Immature* (Grand Rapids, MI: Zondervan, 2014).

5. E. James Wilder et al., *Joy Starts Here: The Transformation Zone* (Lexington, KY: The Shepherd's House, Inc., 2013), 8.

6. Jim Wilder and I define maturity as "suffering well" or "enduring hardship well" in Marcus Warner and Jim Wilder, *Rare Leadership: 4 Uncommon Habits for Increasing Trust, Joy, and Engagement in the People You Lead* (Chicago: Moody Publishers, 2016), 26.

7. *The KJV New Testament Greek Lexicon*, s.v. "Makrothumia," Biblestudy tools.com, accessed February 18, 2022, https://www.biblestudytools.com/lexicons/greek/kjv/makrothumia.html.

8. Warner and Wilder, *Rare Leadership*.

CHAPTER 2: HEART-FOCUSED DISCIPLESHIP

1. Max Lucado, "Six Hours One Friday — Season 1: Hurricane Warnings," Facebook video, 7:17, March 18, 2019, https://www.facebook.com/watch/?v=2312124165690792.

CHAPTER 3: DISCIPLESHIP ON THE BACK OF A NAPKIN

1. To be born of water and the Spirit is most likely a reference to our new birth through baptism and the anointing of the Spirit.

2. BR Ministries, "Why an Egyptian Jew Chose Jesus Christ—George Bebawi," video, 55:38, March 11, 2015, https://www.youtube.com/watch?v=nqyoL0EzDzc&ab_channel=BRMinistries.

CHAPTER 4: DEALING WITH THE WOUNDS OF THE PAST

1. Neil T. Anderson, *The Bondage Breaker: Overcoming Negative Thoughts, Irrational Feelings, Habitual Sins* (Eugene, OR: Harvest House Publishers, 2000), 214–257. See also Neil T. Anderson, *The Steps to Freedom in Christ: A Biblical Guide to Help You Resolve Personal and Spiritual Conflicts and Become a Fruitful Disciple of Jesus* (Bloomington, MN: Bethany House, 2017).

2. Ancestral sin refers to the consequences caused by the sins and iniquities of prior generations that are still affecting us today. In a warfare sense, these consequences can include additional access to influence our environment and behavior.

3. William D. Backus, *The Hidden Rift with God* (Bloomington, MN: Bethany House, 1990).

4. Anonymous prayer cited in Marcus Warner, *Understanding the Wounded Heart* (Carmel, IN: Deeper Walk International, 2019), 75.

5. These strategies for healing are adapted from Warner, *Understanding the Wounded Heart.*

6. Text message to the author, October 4, 2021.

7. The REAL prayer is adapted from *Understanding the Wounded Heart,* 155–159. See also the companion booklet by Marcus Warner, *REAL Prayer: A Guide to Emotional Healing* (Carmel, IN: Deeper Walk International, 2011).

8. Johanna Michaelsen, *The Beautiful Side of Evil* (Eugene, OR: Harvest House Publishers, 1982).

CHAPTER 5: FREEDOM THROUGH SPIRITUAL WARFARE

1. Philip Schaff, *Latin Christianity: Its Founder, Tertullian,* The Early Church Fathers Collection: The Ante Nicene Fathers, vol. 3, ed. Allan Menzies (Grand Rapids, MI: Wm. B. Eerdmans Publishing Co., 2009).

2. Text message forwarded to the author on August 9, 2020.

3. This is a story my father used to tell when teaching on spiritual warfare. I do not know the origin of it.

4. Thus, Paul warns us not to fall into the devil's snares (1 Tim. 3:7; 6:9). He also taught that helping people find freedom from these snares is part of the work of God's servants (2 Tim. 2:24–26).

5. Karl I. Payne, *Spiritual Warfare: Christians, Demonization, and Deliverance* (Alexandria, VA: Republic Book Publishers, 2011).

6. There is such a thing as astral theology, which studies how God uses the stars to communicate to humans. Astral theology is different from astrology, which seeks guidance for life from the stars rather than God. An example of astral theology can be found in Revelation 12:1–2. These verses provide a perfect portrait of what the night sky looked like on September 11, 3 BC. The king planet (Jupiter) and the king star (Regulus) appeared next to each other in the constellation Leo (the Lion), symbolizing that a king was born to the tribe of Judah. Beneath this constellation was Virgo (the Virgin), with the sun appearing where her belly or womb would have been and the moon at her feet. Beneath this constellation was another known to the ancient world as the dragon. Magi from the East could easily have interpreted these signs. In this passage, John appears to be describing a message in the stars from the night of Christ's birth. See Michael Heiser, "The Date of Christ's Birth in Revelation 12," video, 9:35, September 27, 2018, https://www.youtube.com/watch?v=oQsPHvRNYSs.

7. See the article by Christopher Daly, "How Woodrow Wilson's Propaganda Machine Changed American Journalism," *Smithsonian Magazine*, April 28, 2017, https://www.smithsonianmag.com/history/how-woodrow-wilsons-propaganda-machine-changed-american-journalism-180963082/.

CHAPTER 6: IDENTITY IN CHRIST

1. Bob George, *Classic Christianity: Life's Too Short to Miss the Real Thing* (Eugene, OR: Harvest House Publishers, 1989), 41.
2. The story shared here was inspired by a devotional from Dr. Bill Atwood's book, *A Banquet Seat and a Listening Ear: Stories from the Kingdom Frontiers* (Frisco, TX: Ekklesia Society, 2019), 12–20.
3. E. Randolph Richards and Brandon J. O'Brien, *Misreading Scripture with Western Eyes: Removing Cultural Blinders to Better Understand the Bible* (Downers Grove, IL: InterVarsity Press, 2012), 164–165.
4. William Barclay, *Barclay on the Lectionary, Mark: Year B* (Edinburgh: St Andrew Press, 2014) 153–158.
5. See BR Ministries, "Chief Shoefoot—Shaman Testimony," video, 54:47, August 4, 2016, https://www.youtube.com/watch?v=aHK4Irp_pUE, and other videos about his life. See also Mark Andrew Ritchie, *Spirit of the Rainforest: A Yanomamo Shaman's Story* (Island Lake, IL: Island Lake Press, 2000).
6. BR Ministries, "I'll Never Go Back—Shaman Testimony," video, 54:47, February 8, 2013, https://www.youtube.com/watch?v=QW-l-CPC6QY.
7. In the Old Testament the word for temple prostitute is either *qedeshah* for a female prostitute or *qedesh* for a male prostitute. Both words come from *qadosh* which means "holy" or "sacred." See also "Prostitution in the Bible," American Bible Society Resources, https://bibleresources.americanbible.org/resource/prostitution-in-the-bible, which states, "A second kind of prostitute, often called a 'sacred' or 'temple' prostitute, was a female or a male who had sex with worshipers of a god or goddess in a temple."

CHAPTER 7: THE OTHER HALF OF IDENTITY

1. Marcus Warner and Jim Wilder, *Rare Leadership: 4 Uncommon Habits for Increasing Trust, Joy, and Engagement in the People You Lead* (Chicago: Moody Publishers, 2016). See page 37 for a more extensive list.
2. "An Interview with Dr. Allan Schore," *The Science of Psychotherapy*, July 14, 2014, https://www.thescienceofpsychotherapy.com/an-interview-with-allan-schore/.

3. This story is also shared in Deeper Walk Institute, "Course 1, Heart-Focused Discipleship—Session 3: Understanding Law vs. Grace," video, 42:52, December 29, 2021, https://www.youtube.com/watch?v=YsAMhb1TJfQ.

4. James G. Friesen et al., *The Life Model: Living from the Heart Jesus Gave You: The Essentials of Christian Living* (Lexington, KY: The Shepherd's House, Inc., 1999).

5. Marcus Warner, "Understanding the Wounded Heart—Session 1: The Core Model," video, 18:14, December 1, 2020, https://www.youtube.com/watch?v=XMf28gA1zTg&ab_channel=DeeperWalkInternational.

CHAPTER 8: SPIRIT AND SCRIPTURE

1. Corrie Ten Boom (@CorrieTenBoom), "If you look at the world, you'll be distressed. If you look within, you'll be depressed. If you look at God, you'll be at rest," Twitter, July 9, 2009, https://twitter.com/CorrieTenBoom/status/2552264968. This is widely attributed to Corrie ten Boom, although an original source could not be found.

2. Textual date—1876 BC.

3. Textual date—1446 BC.

4. Most likely happened in the 990s.

5. Exile happened in waves: 606, 597, 586. Return happened in 538. Temple rebuilt 516 BC.

6. Jesus was likely born in 3 BC.

CHAPTER 9: LIVING IN THE SPIRIT

1. The Hebrew word *yada* generally means to know someone relationally or experientially, but in this context seems to imply intimacy.

2. E. James Wilder et al., *Joy Starts Here: The Transformation Zone* (Lexington, KY: The Shepherd's House, Inc., 2013), 147–149, 260.

3. E. James Wilder et al., *Joyful Journey: Listening to Immanuel* (Los Angeles: Presence and Practice, 2020), 13.

4. *Hesed* is normally transliterated *chesed*, but I find that confusing to people who don't know Hebrew. So I have opted for simpler spelling.

5. Mark I. Bubeck, *Prayer Patterns for Revival* (Chicago: Moody Publishers, 2020).

6. Judy Dunagan, *The Loudest Roar: Living in the Unshakable Victory of Christ* (Chicago: Moody Publishers, 2022). At the time of writing this book, Judy sits on the board of Deeper Walk International.

7. Neil T. Anderson, *Liberating Prayer: Finding Freedom by Connecting with God* (Eugene, OR: Harvest House Publishers, 2012).

8. A. W. Tozer, *The Pursuit of God* (Chicago: Moody Publishers, 2015), 88.

CHAPTER 10: HEART-FOCUSED COMMUNITY

1. Written testimonial in Deeper Walk online small group, October 19, 2020.

2. Jim Wilder and Michel Hendricks, *The Other Half of Church: Christian Community, Brain Science, and Overcoming Spiritual Stagnation* (Chicago: Moody Publishers, 2020).

3. The word *hesed* is usually transliterated as *chesed*, to show that the word starts with a hard "h" sound. So, if you are used to seeing it the other way, it is the same word and a legitimate alternative to the transliteration process.

4. Marcus Warner and Jim Wilder, *Rare Leadership in the Workplace: 4 Uncommon Habits that Improve Focus, Engagement, and Productivity* (Chicago: Northfield Publishing, 2021), 48.

5. The term *upside-down maturity* was coined by Anne Bierling while working with Dr. Wilder at Shepherd's House counseling center in Pasadena.

6. E. James Wilder, *The Complete Guide to Living with Men* (Lexington, KY: Shepherd's House, Inc., 2004). Sadly, as of the writing of this book, *The Complete Guide to Living with Men* is out of print.

7. Jim Wilder, email message to the author, August 2019.

8. Amy Hamilton Brown, *Journey Groups: Level One: A Relational Discipleship Experience* (Carmel, IN: Deeper Walk International, 2021). At the time of this writing, level two curriculum is expected to be released in late 2023.

CHAPTER 11: MISSION

1. Lee's story was made into a movie called *The Case for Christ* that is available on several streaming services at the time this book is being written.

2. Lauren Sturdy, "Strobel encourages Texas Baptists to 'make people thirst for God,'" *Baptist Standard*, November 16, 2016, accessed February 17, 2022, https://www.baptiststandard.com/news/texas/strobel-encourages-texas-baptists-to-make-people-thirst-for-god/.

3. Ibid.

4. The content of the REAL Prayer booklet can be found in the book *Understanding the Wounded Heart* (Carmel, IN: Deeper Walk International, 2019). See also the companion booklet by *REAL Prayer: A Guide to Emotional Healing*.

TAKE YOUR NEXT STEP

deeperwalkinternational.org

Resources & Training in Heart-Focused Discipleship

*Visit our website for a free companion video e-course
to this book, plus other free resources today.*

"What comes into our minds when we think about God is the most important thing about us."
—A. W. Tozer

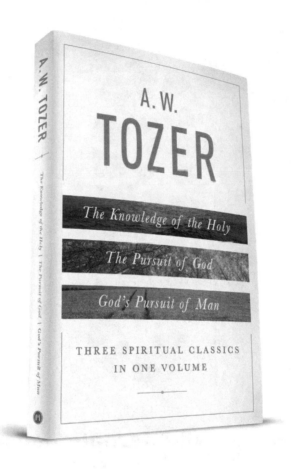

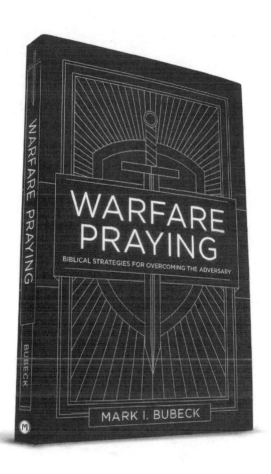